AIMING FOR AN A
IN A-LEVEL
RELIGIOUS
STUDIES

Julian Waterfield

HODDER
EDUCATION
AN HACHETTE UK COMPANY

Acknowledgements

Every effort has been made to trace all copyright holders, but if any have been inadvertently overlooked, the Publishers will be pleased to make the necessary arrangements at the first opportunity.

Although every effort has been made to ensure that website addresses are correct at time of going to press, Hodder Education cannot be held responsible for the content of any website mentioned in this book. It is sometimes possible to find a relocated web page by typing in the address of the home page for a website in the URL window of your browser.

Hachette UK's policy is to use papers that are natural, renewable and recyclable products and made from wood grown in well-managed forests and other controlled sources. The logging and manufacturing processes are expected to conform to the environmental regulations of the country of origin.

Orders: please contact Bookpoint Ltd, 130 Park Drive, Milton Park, Abingdon, Oxon OX14 4SE. Telephone: (44) 01235 827720. Fax: (44) 01235 400401. Email education@bookpoint.co.uk Lines are open from 9 a.m. to 5 p.m., Monday to Saturday, with a 24-hour message answering service. You can also order through our website: www.hoddereducation.co.uk

ISBN: 978 1 5104 4920 6

© Julian Waterfield 2019

First published in 2019 by
Hodder Education,
An Hachette UK Company
Carmelite House
50 Victoria Embankment
London EC4Y 0DZ

www.hoddereducation.co.uk

Impression number   10 9 8 7 6 5 4 3 2 1

Year   2023   2022   2021   2020   2019

Typeset by Integra Software Services Pvt. Ltd., Pondicherry, India

Printed in India

A catalogue record for this title is available from the British Library.

Contents

Getting the most from this book

Aiming for an A is designed to help you master the skills you need to achieve the highest grades.

The following features will help you get the most from this book:

Learning objectives

> A summary of the skills that will be covered in the chapter.

 Exam tip

Practical advice about how to apply your skills to the exam.

Activity

An opportunity to test your skills with practical activities.

! Common pitfall

Problem areas where candidates often miss out on marks.

The difference between...

Explanations of key differences that make A-grade students stand out.

Annotated example

Exemplar answers with commentary showing how to achieve top grades.

Take it further

Suggestions for further reading or activities that will stretch your thinking.

You should know

> A summary of key points to take away from the chapter.

About this book

Religious studies is an exciting, vibrant subject. It combines the ancient discipline of philosophy with the current challenges of ethics. You study the developments and impacts of a religion from origins to contemporary application. It is an all-encompassing subject that touches on many other disciplines that you might be studying for your other A-levels.

With that excitement comes a number of challenges. You need to develop different skills in different modules. You might not be interested in every topic that you study but you need to be able to answer questions on them all. This book will help you to develop the underlying skills that will guide you through the 2-year course — and it is important to remember that the course is a marathon, not a sprint. If you are reading this as you start the course, you might still be reeling from the shock of just how much harder A-level is than GCSE, and to top it all off, religious studies is unlikely to be your only subject.

Your mindset

Your college or school will address what it expects a learner's attitude or 'mindset' to be. It is important to follow every piece of advice you are given if only to avoid conflict with the authorities (whatever example you think Jesus, Bonhoeffer or liberation theology may give). However, simply following advice is not going to help you to make the step up to A-level. This is where you really do come in as a fully empowered learner.

You should be careful to adopt a 'growth' rather than a 'fixed' mindset. In a nutshell, this means that your approach must be ever ready to adapt, change and develop (growth mindset) rather than to think narrowly, in black and white or in 'it's always been done' terms (fixed mindset). The idea is that our ability and intelligence are not fixed but can be developed — there is always a next step.

Being in control

You need to be in control of your decision making and how you choose to apply yourself to the college or school framework. You need to be clear on your goals, work out the energy you wish to put into them and then make them happen. The goals you set should be SMART:

→ **Specific** — don't set general goals like 'get an A', set really narrow ones to do with mastering a topic or sub-topic, or a skill.
→ **Measurable** — be able to measure when you have achieved your goal.
→ **Achievable** — be realistic and clear about how your goal will be achieved.
→ **Relevant** — check that your goal is necessary.
→ **Time-bound** — set yourself a certain timeframe in which to achieve your goal.

For example, when revising, you could set yourself the target of getting better at the Cosmological Argument topic. A SMART version of this could be: 'Improve my notes on the Cosmological Argument by adding information from the textbook before the end of half term so that I can learn better from them.'

Being reflective

The best students are those who are reflective. They are constantly trying to adapt, change and better themselves. They look for role models, never say no to advice and develop good habits — if you have studied virtue ethics, you will see the similarities. However, these habits do not come without setbacks.

Academically, you will try things that do not work and feel that you have wasted time reading a book or writing something in a particular way. Don't forget to see the big picture and to remember that time spent refining your overall techniques is never time wasted.

At the same time, life in general will throw you curve balls over the 2 years and it is important to work out how you are going to roll with it, bounce back, grow as a person and maintain your study habits.

The reflective learner is relentlessly positive, uses every opportunity to improve (and every tool out there, including people) and is very much looking forward to the journey.

Grades and levels

Much is made of grade boundaries by both students and teachers but spending too much time thinking about these is an example of a fixed mindset rather than a growth one. Not only do the grade boundaries change each year, they also change in line with the other papers that you sit so that if one paper is harder than the others in a given year, then the boundaries will be differently weighted. Trying to second-guess what the boundaries will be next summer or even the summer after will do nothing for your final result.

In addition, the way that marks are awarded each summer is decided only after everyone has sat their exams. Therefore, the examiners can adjust how they mark depending on various external factors in order to be as fair to the students as possible. This means that marking is never an exact science in a subject that is assessed by essay — there is no such thing as a 'right mark' in religious studies. The best you and your teacher can do is to be as realistic as possible when marking and use essay marks as a tool along the journey to try to improve for next time — a growth mindset.

Essays are assessed by 'levels of response'. An essay is first read, then judged to be in a certain level (or band) and then a mark from within that band is awarded. The levels are made up of different descriptors which outline the characteristics of an essay at that level. The marker needs to try to match what they have read to those descriptors. There is more about this in Chapter 3 on essay writing.

Assessment objectives

Assessment objectives (AOs) focus on the core skills that are assessed in your religious studies exams. You need to gain marks for each AO in different ways. We shall see how AOs are judged and how they are tested as the book goes on. For now, you need to be clear what each AO is, as described in the table below.

Assessment objective	Description	What type of learning is required
AO1 (40% of total mark)	Demonstrate knowledge and understanding of religion and belief, including: • religious, philosophical and/or ethical thought and teaching • influence of beliefs, teachings and practices on individuals, societies and communities • cause and significance of similarities and differences in belief, teaching and practice • approaches to the study of religion and belief.	• Recall of information and arguments. • Relating information to different aspects of the course. • Understanding who, what, where, why, when and how. • Application to modern or everyday life. • Ability to explain, interpret, summarise and compare.
AO2 (60% of total mark)	Analyse and evaluate aspects of, and approaches to, religion and belief, including their significance, influence and study.	• Ability to take explanations deeper, using own ideas and deep thinking. • Ability to make links and return to the big picture. • Ability to balance ideas and viewpoints and reach your own judgement.

As more marks are awarded for AO2, it is tempting to think that the groundwork of AO1 requires less effort during the course. The reality, however, is that the basics are always needed and the number of marks for AO2 simply demonstrates the need for you to be able to write a superbly argued, clear essay when required. Not arguing well in an essay can slice several grades off a mark in a flash but your AO1 skills make up the building blocks of the whole essay.

Exam boards

Although the final section of this book looks at the different quirks of the exam boards, it is worth making yourself familiar with what your board offers. On the appropriate website for your board, you will find several different resources, some of which are listed in the table below.

Exam board resource	Use for the student
Specification	This document takes you through all that you will need to know (including all the optional papers). Make sure you are looking at the A-level specification and not the AS one. Questions cannot be set on topics that don't appear in this document.
Sample assessment materials	These are the initial sample question papers and their mark schemes that were written when the specification was first published. They set out the format of the questions in the exam and the criteria against which your answers are marked.
Past papers	Usually, exam boards keep the most recent paper in a secure area so that teachers can use them for mock exams. Remember that if a question has come up before, it cannot come up with the same wording again.
Examiners' reports	These reports by the senior examiners highlight the key strengths and weaknesses of that year's set of exam entries. They contain a potential treasure chest of advice — tips that have been written while the marking is still fresh in the mind of the examiners.
Candidate exemplars	These are actual candidate answers that are provided with a commentary from an examiner. They are a key way of trying to understand the thought process of your eventual marker.

How to use this book

The different chapters in this book explore the different skills required for A-level religious studies. There is some overlap between them, so it is not a bad idea to skim over the chapters to get a sense of what comes where. You can read bits as they become relevant (e.g. before your next essay) or you can dip in and out a bit at a time. You might like to revisit the key areas every once in a while, to refresh yourself — or to reassure yourself that you are working well.

The book starts by looking at the three areas that are integral to A-level religious studies — note-taking, reading skills and essay writing — before moving on to think about the exam itself.

→ Chapter 1 provides an overview of the 2-year course. It explores some of the basics that will help you through it, most notably note-taking.

→ Chapter 2 explores different types of reading and how to decide what to read. It will teach you effective ways to read, the pitfalls to avoid and how reading can enhance the whole course.

→ Chapter 3 moves on to writing skills. This is a key chapter in helping you to succeed in your exams because writing is the way that you are assessed in the subject. Of course, that success won't come from picking up this chapter the week before your final A-levels.

→ Chapter 4 looks at revision techniques you can use both during the course and in the final revision period. It tries to give a variety of approaches so that you can find what works best for you.

→ Chapter 5 gives advice on how to prepare for the exams and how to approach the exam itself.

→ The final section ensures that you have a real sense of what your exam board's assessment looks like. It gives specific tips for the different boards.

Reading this book is not going to get you an A or an A* on its own. It will, however, give you some indication of what typifies a top-grade student. And it will serve as an accompaniment to good teaching, an excellent learner mindset and a developing love for the subject.

1 The journey

Learning objectives

> To reflect on ways to study across the 2-year course
> To consider who can help you on your way
> To develop your own style for taking notes

The big picture

Your religious studies A-level is a 2-year journey or process, with the focus on the two or three long exams at the end of the course. Everything you do during the course needs to be guided by that as everything you do is aiming towards a period of revision followed by two or three critical points in time.

Two years seems like a long time, of course, but the process of aiming for the top grades needs careful attention throughout the course. You need time to find your voice in writing essays, time to make mistakes in various techniques and then to find a method that will work and so on.

During your course you may well have more than one teacher and you will be studying philosophy, ethics and a religion. Make sure that you continue to find links between the different parts of the course — after 2 years, you will find that links fall into place.

You will also be studying other subjects. While this book has study skills that will help you in religious studies, some of the core skills will be ones you use in other subjects and it is likely that you will use similar techniques in all your subjects. Your time pressures will be determined by those other subjects as well as by your desire for a work–life balance.

! Common pitfall

If you realise that the way you studied in the first few months of the course was wrong, don't forget to go back and update your notes, taking into account the lessons you have learned. If you don't do this and one of the early topics comes up in the exam, you will find yourself a step behind.

Activity

Map out a typical week during term time. When do you schedule rest and relaxation time? How much time during the week do you have for work? Don't forget study periods at school or college and to allow a realistic amount of time for home study.

Alongside your studies, you will probably also be trying to work out what you are going to do next in your life. Be open to the possibility of taking any of your A-level subjects on to university — don't underestimate the power of studying a purely academic subject at university rather than taking a 'career' course. As you go through the first year of your A-levels, you will soon realise which of the three or four subjects you are studying is the one you look forward to the most and the one for which you read around the subject most willingly.

Who can help you?

Although Kant might be disappointed, it is important to use the people around you to the best of your ability and theirs. Everybody's situation is different but perhaps there are some ideas in what follows that you could adopt.

Your teacher

Whether your course is being delivered by one, two or three teachers or lecturers, this is the most valuable resource that you have available to you. Teachers desperately want their students to do well and this is particularly so at A-level where you, the student, have opted to study the subject that they have dedicated their careers to — you will often get more time from them than younger students might. So, first and foremost, ask your teacher when you have a query or when you come across something you do not understand.

Your teachers will very likely pepper their lessons with suggestions of things to read, avenues to follow or ways to stretch yourself. The top-grade students will be those who pursue those suggestions — and who find other routes (e.g. by going to a website suggested by a teacher and then using that website to follow links to others). It is important to remember that there is no 'official list' of useful books or websites a teacher might suggest. Success comes from many different sources.

The most valuable advice that teachers will offer will be feedback on your written work. Using feedback well can be the equivalent of spending an additional 6 months in the classroom. Good feedback is designed to take you one step further at a time, so be patient and improve one thing in each essay. Table 1.1 gives some examples of useful feedback and what you could do in response.

Table 1.1 Using teacher feedback wisely

Feedback	Possible response
Good/excellent	Ensure you know why it was a good paragraph or section and try to mimic that style in the future.
Develop/explain	If you are unsure of how your point could have been developed, make sure you refer to your notes, the textbook or your teacher to find out why. If the information isn't in your notes, make sure you add it in.
Argument unclear	Rewrite the section, the paragraph or even the entire essay and ask your teacher to look at the improved version.
Incorrect	Make sure you review the information to ensure you get it correct next time. If your notes are not up-to-date, make sure they become so.
Essay was too short	Go back to your notes and the textbook and make sure that you know how to write more next time. How good was your essay plan? If you didn't fully understand the question, ask your teacher for help.
Essay was too long	Look to see how you could have written the essay more concisely without losing the detail you included. How good was your essay plan? Try rewriting a paragraph to experiment.

Your classmates

Your classmates are all on the same journey as you, and you can be a wonderful resource to each other, although it is important not to be a burden on each other, too. Some classes successfully set up social media groups to discuss things out of class or share materials they have found. Others enjoy talking about the lessons in the common room or over lunch. If you find someone who is also aiming for the top grades, then you can help to push each other further.

Don't forget that if you are in the first year of the course, students in the year above are a year ahead of you on the journey. They might be able to provide you with help and support or just talk you through a topic you're struggling with.

People at home

Friends and family at home can help by testing you on topics, asking what you've been studying or asking silly questions to make you explain something more clearly. If you can explain something at the dinner table then you really do understand it! But not only that, if your family talks about the world around you, you will begin to draw links between what they are talking about and the courses you are following.

Note-taking

The process of taking notes is a daily task for the A-level student. Notes ensure that you:

→ are processing what you are reading or hearing

→ do not have to return to the original source

→ have material to revise from for tests and exams

Keep these purposes in mind as you work and make sure that you leave nothing to chance — will you remember what you chose not to write down in 18 months' time?

The first rule of taking notes is never to write things down as they appear in front of you or to treat your teacher's comments as dictation. It is important to engage actively in lessons so that you can develop the higher skills of analysis required for the top marks.

Once you have left a lesson, your notes will need to be enhanced by additional notes from your own reading, especially your textbook. See Chapter 2 on reading skills for more information about this, but for now, make sure that you leave space in your notes to add things in.

What should your notes look like?

Ultimately, this is up to you. Whether you create mind maps or use bullet points, handwrite them or type them, it is only you that needs to use them in the end. They should be legible but cutting corners with spelling, punctuation and grammar is quite usual.

Notes should contain more than just AO1 material. If you find bias in a source or in the views of the scholar, this is appropriate material to include. Some students like to use a range of colours to highlight different types of information, but it is helpful to be consistent.

> **! Common pitfall**
>
> Don't simply write out your teacher's PowerPoint presentation without engaging with the material. Remember that your teacher is likely to be saying things in their own words while they give their presentation and the combination of the PowerPoint material and the explanation is what should appear in your notes.

How your notes are organised is, again, a personal matter, but adding page numbers and the date you made the notes is a useful start. If you are using a computer, make sure that the folders and filenames you use are logical and not just the default filename of the first few words of the document.

One technique that some students find useful is to divide a piece of A4 lined notepaper into different sections before you start and use it as shown in Figure 1.1.

Date — topic — page number

Here you write the main part of your notes.

Here you write questions that come out of the notes or things you want to follow up.

Here you write a summary of the key information and arguments that can be found on the page.

Figure 1.1 Example of a method of note-taking

Take it further

The system of notes shown in Figure 1.1 is similar to the Cornell method. You could look up this system on the internet to explore the reasoning behind it and ways of making it work.

Many people choose to use shorthand symbols to help them to take notes at speed. Table 1.2 on the next page may give you some ideas about symbols to use.

> **! Common pitfall**
>
> You may begin by taking notes in an exercise book, but the fixed pages do not allow for the more dynamic approach to note-taking that A-levels generally require.

Table 1.2 Some useful symbols and abbreviations

Symbol/abbreviation	Meaning	Symbol/abbreviation	Meaning
=	equals	∴	therefore
≠	does not equal	∵ or b/c	because
>	is greater than	cf or cp	compare (with/to)
<	is less than	i.e.	that is
→	leads to	θ	theology
↔	links to	φ	philosophy
e.g.	for example	ψ	psychology
c̄ or w/	with	Xtn (Xty)	Christian(ity)
c̄out or w/out	without	Bs/Hs/Ms/Ss	Buddhists, Hindus, Muslims, Sikhs

End-of-topic notes

Absolutely central to success at the highest level is to leave each topic properly 'wrapped up' when you finish it and not to wait for a revision period to pull it all together.

When you finish a topic, you will have your class notes, notes from the textbook and notes from your wider reading. You need to be sure that you have consolidated these into one final set of notes that you will use when it comes to learning the topic for a test and then at the end of the course. These notes should cover everything in a logical order and should take into account all of the advice you have been given in your written work as well as the information from the various resources. If done well, you won't need to get your old notes out again (but keep them safe in a separate file, just in case). This isn't to say that you might not need to add to end-of-topic notes as you go through the course and make new links, but it really is best practice to create a final set. We will see how these end-of-topic notes can become revision notes in Chapter 5.

Don't forget that if you use your notes to learn for a test and you don't do as well as you had hoped, you may need to update those notes for next time.

You should know

> How to see your studies in the context of a 2-year course while studying several subjects.
> The importance of using your teacher to help you push towards the next level, especially using his or her feedback.
> How to take good notes and ways you could do this.
> The importance of having good end-of-topic notes.

2 Reading skills

Learning objectives

> To understand when to use different types of reading and why
> To understand how reading contributes to your overall note-taking
> To know how to deal with set texts
> To know how to read the extracts from the anthology in the Edexcel exam

The main reason you need to sit and read is to develop your understanding of your religious studies A-level course. However, reading is also important for other reasons. If you are going to be successful in your writing, then you need to be clear how central reading is in the process. Reading does not mean simply reading your textbook, nor the occasional chapter of a recommended book from a library; it means that you should read anything and everything. If your A-level subjects are linked, you might find your reading links with your subjects naturally, but reading unrelated texts is just as good and, whether or not you are studying English, reading a fiction book is always a good use of time. The more you read, too, the more your standard of written English will improve.

However, reading for your subject should never be passive. Passive reading does not allow you to think through what you are reading and you are unlikely to retain the information. Active reading, on the other hand, forces you to think critically about what you are engaging with. Always make sure you are in your workspace, with pen and paper to hand so that you can add to your notes and engage fully with the text.

Reasons to read

The most important reason to read is to get to know your subject better. Like all things, it is helpful to have your purpose in mind: why are you reading? Table 2.1 has some possible answers to this question.

Table 2.1 Reasons to read during your A-levels

Reason to read	Description
To write a particular essay	Here you might use your textbook and a few particular websites or other books that you use regularly.
To fill in the gaps of something you didn't quite understand	Again, your textbook will be important but other books like revision guides or websites written by teachers will help here.
To prepare your end-of-topic notes	Make sure you use all the resources supplied by your teacher for this. Spend some time on the internet looking up the topic and see what you find.
To 'read around' the topic	Here you are trying to broaden your understanding of a topic beyond A-level resources.
To broaden your experience of the subject	You might do this when you want to go beyond the material in the A-level specification.
Just to read	You might do this for fun, or to fill in the gaps in your day.

Reading for an essay

If you have been set an essay to do at home, you will of course need to use more than just your class notes to write it. If you are working smartly, the purpose of reading at this stage is two-fold. First, you are trying to prepare for a particular essay title — a relatively narrow focus. You may be looking at how Kant is applied to an aspect of practical ethics, for example. Second, you can use this opportunity to expand your notes on the topic as a whole. How Kant is applied to other areas of practical ethics not only helps you prepare for the final exam but also shows you Kant in action.

The textbook

Your textbook is likely to be your first port of call for an essay, if you didn't use it in class. Textbooks have often been written by examiners and/or experts in teaching the subject at A-level and so they are the perfect place to start.

When reading the textbook, the ultimate aim should be not to have to re-read the chapter at a later date. If you are in good study habits, you will be making notes from the textbook that can be added to your class notes, later consolidating them into one set of end-of-topic notes. Much of the material in the textbook will hopefully be the same as in class and so you can concentrate on analysing what you are reading and deciding:

→ if it could be phrased more usefully

→ if there are case studies, quotations or examples worth noting

→ if it gives a bit more detail than you got in class

Textbooks often give you pointers to further books or resources that you can use, usually at the end of chapters, so you can use this as a way in to reading around the subject. They are also full of activities and discussion points that take you a step further. Taking time to stop and think these through — or even to answer the questions — is a very good use of time.

Other books and websites

As you go through the course, you will find other books and websites that you really like using. Some of these might be written

> **! Common pitfall**
>
> If you prepare only for the essay title that has been set, you will find that your notes are unbalanced at the end of the process. Time taken during the course to widen your reading and note-taking will save time at the revision stage and will enhance your overall understanding early on in the process.

by academics, some by teachers and others by other students. It is good practice to keep a record of these in a mini-bibliography at the front of your file so that you do not lose track of the ones you like. Once more, any new information from this material needs to be added to your overall notes, rather than making new sets of notes that repeat information or make your notes too cumbersome.

Table 2.2 explores how and why you might use websites written by different people.

Table 2.2 Website authorship

Author	Benefits	Challenges
Written by academics	• Experts in their fields • Sometimes, they are the people you are actually studying	• May use difficult language which needs careful consideration • Don't run before you can walk: sometimes it is better to use other resources first until you understand the topic well enough
Written by teachers	• Experts at communicating with your age group • Understand the requirements of the course	• Might be writing for a different exam board with different emphases • Might just be 'more of the same', similar material to your class notes and textbook
Written by students	• May have been through the same struggles as you • Might be in a familiar style	• Material may not be accurate • Might not give any new information

When using websites, it is important to make sure that you stop looking for new material when you are confident you understand the topic and have covered everything. There is no point in repeating yourself again and again. Get going on the essay and come back to reading only if you discover a need to do so.

Reading to fill in gaps

In any A-level subject, but especially in a complex one such as religious studies, you will find some topics harder than others. This is normal. Reading can fill in the gaps where you don't quite understand a topic. You may have asked your teacher the same question over and over and the way that they explain it just doesn't quite work for you. Again, you might use other books and websites, rather than your class notes and textbook, but the goal is different. Here you are looking for specific information to increase your understanding. When the gap in your knowledge has been filled in, move on.

Reading to make end-of-topic notes

As we saw in Chapter 1, success comes from making really good, final notes on each topic so that you don't need to update them as the course goes on. Whether or not you have been set an essay on a topic or sub-topic, it is important to prepare these notes, using reading, as you go through the course. Class notes, the textbook, other books and websites can all be used but there is also the opportunity to be a bit more flexible in the resources you choose.

! Common pitfall

Make sure that the websites you use are not extreme, faith-based websites. Always look for balance and always double-check any new information with a second source, your textbook or your teacher.

Activity

Go through your notes on the topics you have studied so far and, on the front page of each set, rate yourself on how complete you think your knowledge is. You can give yourself a mark out of 5 or use a red/amber/green system. When you have filled in any gaps in those sections, you can change your rating.

Search engines

Using your favourite search engine can open up doors and ideas in the subject. Spending time searching for things and then following links as they come up can be an excellent use of time, as long as your reading remains active, not passive.

The key here is to be critical about what you are reading and to be clear about the bias of the websites that you are using. In religious studies, you will encounter a number of websites that are written from faith standpoints that might be closer to sermons than academic texts. Try enhancing your search by using some of the following techniques:

→ Use double quotation marks to search for the exact text of a specific phrase (e.g. "design argument" returns pages with that complete phrase in, rather than any page with 'design' and 'argument' used in different sentences).

→ Refine your search using the names of scholars (e.g. "design argument", "paley").

→ Look for specific aspects of a topic (e.g. "design argument", "weaknesses").

→ Look for pages written for academic students (e.g. "design argument", "study notes" or "design argument", "A-level").

→ Look for pages written for your exam board (e.g. "design argument", "OCR").

→ Use the search tools to narrow your search to recent pages (e.g. "euthanasia", selecting 'past year').

→ Use the search tools to narrow your search to the UK (e.g. "euthanasia arguments", selecting 'pages from the UK').

A01 or A02?

At this stage in your reading, you will be clearer about what skills you need in order to do well in a particular topic or sub-topic. You therefore need to be clear what you are trying to get out of your reading and make sure the two match.

A01 reading

Here you are reading in order to develop your knowledge about the topic. You want to know something or understand it. Use materials developed specifically for your exam board — your textbook or specific revision sites — as a starting point and then be absolutely clear what you want to type into your search engine, or to find in a book. Then, ensure your notes precisely cover all the knowledge required by the specification. This is an active process and it avoids you falling into the trap of simply copying out a section of a topic passively.

A02 reading

In this type of reading you are focused on how different scholars analyse and evaluate a topic. You are hoping to develop your own critical analysis and evaluation skills. The subtext here is to be able to read the work of a scholar and identify their argument and how they build it (see annotated example 2.1). If you find that daunting, first see if you can do it with an essay written by a friend — or find a website that has sample essays on it to use.

Activity

Take the topic you are studying at the moment and practise your search engine skills. When you have found a page, consider what the author's standpoint is and how that will affect how you view the material on the page.

! Common pitfall

You may think that reading a textbook and identifying the strengths and weaknesses of an argument is A02 reading. However, all that does is help you to **know and understand** the strengths and weaknesses of an argument — which is an A01 skill. However, 60% of the marks in A-level religious studies are awarded for your ability to **analyse and evaluate**, an A02 skill.

Annotated example 2.1

This sample text has been annotated to show you how you can identify an argument in your reading to develop your AO2 skills of analysis and evaluation.

The passage is taken from *An Introduction to Buddhism: Teachings, History and Practices* by Peter Harvey, Cambridge University Press, 1990, p. 46.

Reproduced by permission of Cambridge University Press.

Path of Buddhism

'While' is a useful indicator that the paragraph is reaching a judgement that is worth analysing.

The argument stated is made forcefully but calmly. The paragraph goes on to build the argument gradually.

Relevant knowledge (AO1) is given to justify the argument but its place within the argument is clear to see.

'Thus' indicates a conclusion at the end of a series of points to make the argument and thus reach an evaluative judgement. The argument is that the path of Buddhism is a gradual process, rather than a black-and-white set of beliefs.

The argument's development in this sentence is an example of analysis.

The analysis is completed with a concluding sentence before moving on to the next point.

While teachings on karma and belief are an important part of Buddhist belief, they are not the *most* crucial nor the most specifically Buddhist. They act, though, as the lead up to and motivator for the most important teachings, those on the Four Holy Truths. When teaching lay persons, the Buddha frequently began with a 'step-by-step discourse': (i) on giving and moral observance as leading to a heavenly rebirth, and then, (ii) on the advantages of renouncing sense-pleasures (by meditative calming of the mind). Such teachings were used to inspire his hearers and help them gain a state of mind which was calm, joyful and open. In this state of readiness, they would then be taught the Four Holy Truths relating to suffering.

…

Thus the overall path of Buddhism is seen as a training which gradually moves towards the profounder teachings, just as the ocean bottom shelves down gradually from the shore into the depths.

Reading around the topic

Sometimes your interest will have been sparked by a topic and you will want to delve into it further, perhaps to look at other versions of an argument or to find out about other scholars who have been involved. The A-level specifications are pretty narrow compared with the subject as a whole. For example, you might want to find out about different feminists who have commented on religion, or simply find out more about Mary Daly and her work than the specification calls for.

Alternatively, you may be feeling dissatisfied and you want to find out more about a topic so that you can engage with it better. For example, you might want to learn more about a scholar's background, to better understand where they are coming from.

Search engines are a wonderful way to achieve this, of course, but now might be the time to use more academic books. You can ask your teacher what books they might recommend, look in your school or college library or go to your local library.

Using academic books

When you are focused on a particular topic, you will probably need to be selective about how much of a book you read in order to make the best use of your time. Making use of the contents and the index is a good way to identify the relevant sections. (Of course, if you like the book, there is nothing to stop you reading it all!)

The difference between...

Contents	Index
The contents give the page number of the major chapters (and sometimes the sub-sections) and are found at the start of the book. Contents pages are useful when there is a whole chapter on the topic or person you want to read about but sometimes chapters might be more generally named.	The index lists the key terms, concepts, people or topics that are covered in the book and is found at the end of the book. It is useful for finding mentions of the topic you are looking at in unexpected chapters so that you can make links and understand the context better. Some academic books have more than one index, for example one for people, one for themes and so on.

Be patient with this type of reading. You might spend a fair bit of time just looking at books and finding nothing of interest or nothing new, but this is a normal part of research. Look at the sections below on skimming and scanning to help you through this.

Continue to be active in your reading. When you find something useful, add it to your notes. Consider the type of book you are reading: does it have a bias? You could try having a sheet of paper with a title such as 'Other thoughts' for each topic and you can note down interesting things you found out — or just things that you have thought about while you read.

Broadening your experience

A-grade students are often those who have a real feel for their subject. It doesn't matter if you get obsessed by a particular aspect of the subject or like to keep things broad, it is good to know something about different aspects of the subject beyond that required in the specification. For example, you might be studying Islam as your main religion but also be interested in one of the eastern religions. Alternatively, you might want to explore aspects of ethics that are not on the course.

Another reason you might want to broaden your experience of the subject is if you want to apply for a related subject at university. You might want to mention a book or two in your personal statement or the fact that you have been reading a particular journal regularly. If you are applying to a university that interviews applicants, you will certainly want to be able to talk about the subject more broadly in your interview.

This is the time to read whole books and to look for journals that can support your experience.

Journals

Academic journals are usually quite difficult to come by outside of university libraries. There are some that are written for the A-level student, such as *Dialogue*, *Philosophy Now* and *Religious Studies Review* (which is no longer published but libraries will often have back issues). Specific religious organisations will have magazines and journals from a faith perspective. Ask your school or college librarian what they have both in the library and digitally and see if they have the budget to order one for you if they don't currently have anything.

These journals will contain articles that are specifically about a topic you are studying but often will also have relatively short articles that explore something that is not on your course and which can broaden your appetite for religious studies.

Activity

Find an article in a journal about something you have not studied. Make a flow diagram, highlighting the key arguments in each section of the article to see how the author has written about the topic academically.

Books

Some books will be general introductions to a subject area and will whet your appetite and others will be academic studies. Both will take you out of your comfort zone and so perseverance is the key. There will be styles of writing that you are not used to, but which will reap rewards. They will give you a taste of what studying the subject at university might be like. Ask your teacher for recommendations and use the bibliographies in the textbooks you are using to find further reading. Authors that are popular in the religious studies A-level community include Blackburn, Dawkins, Law, Polkinghorne, Singer and Vardy to name just a few.

Take it further

Look out for some of the following series of books:

- The 'Very Short Introduction' books, published by Oxford University Press.
- The 'Teach yourself' books.

Try to find introductions to different aspects of religious studies, for example:

- Guides to the Old and New Testaments.
- An overview of Christian theology.
- An overview of philosophy of religion.

Just reading

Reading brings its own pleasures and there is always a place for a light storybook beside your bed. Applying the suggestions made above to your other A-level subjects will draw out links to religious studies that you might not have expected. You should always keep on top of the news, through either an online news site or a newspaper (your school or college library may well take a daily newspaper), not just because it will link directly to ethics but because it will broaden your awareness of the world around you. Religious studies is, after all, a study of the world and of people. Reading literature from different cultures or periods of history will also make you think about scholars from similar periods of history or perspectives on faith outside the UK. The main problem will always be that there is not enough time to read everything.

Ways of reading

We have seen how important it is for reading to be active and not passive, forcing your brain to engage with what you are reading. We can break reading down further and consider different approaches for different circumstances.

Skimming

Skimming involves skipping through a text. The aim is to get a general overview to identify the main points so that you can decide if you need to read it more closely. It's the same sort of reading you are likely to do if you look at a television guide to decide what to watch, or when you look at the list of results from a search engine when deciding which site to click on. It gives you a sense of the general purpose of the writer from which you might begin to identify any bias in the text.

You can skim read by:
→ looking at the headings and the sub-headings
→ looking for key words or the author's emphasis which are in bold or italics
→ reading the first sentence of different sections and sometimes the last sentence of a paragraph
→ reading the introduction
→ looking at any pictures, key quotations or charts or tables

It is unlikely that skim reading will ever be the only type of reading you do. You will use it to decide whether to give more time to a particular text. As an active reader, you might note down some key words that come out of the process of skim reading as you go along. Some students find themselves only skim reading, which is not, of course, the way to the higher grades.

Activity

Pick a relevant text to practise skim reading, perhaps a website on a topic you are about to study. When you have finished, note down the key points that came out of it and then check how well you retained the information. Keep practising the skill until it becomes second nature.

Scanning

Scanning is also a form of speed reading and is used when you are looking for particular information. You are, perhaps, trying to find a particular point to fill in a gap in your understanding or you are looking for a quotation to add to your notes to enhance your work on a scholar. You could look for numbers in the text if you are searching for dates or perhaps capital letters to look for names. It is important that before you begin you are clear about what the aim of the exercise is and try to think through what you are looking for — a key word or a quotation. It is also helpful to use your finger as a guide here — run it down the page as you look.

Intensive reading

This is the most important form of reading you will do for your religious studies A-level. Here you are engaging fully with a text and the aim is for you to understand not just the content but also what is *not* written, such as the bias or the context. As a result of intensive reading, you will remember more of the material and you should be able to express it in your own words. As always, make sure the goal of the exercise is clear to you. Are you trying to add to your class notes or to summarise a new argument? You will see this technique in use in the annotated example below.

Annotated example 2.2

This sample text has been annotated to show you how you can engage fully with a text while reading intensively.

The passage is taken from *Practical Ethics* (2nd edition) by Peter Singer, Cambridge University Press, 1993, pp. 135–6.

Reproduced by permission of Cambridge University Press.

It is worth being clear what 'today' means. The book was published in 1993. It should make you think about what has changed since it was written.

This indicates that there is a real debate on this topic that is important to recognise and understand from all perspectives.

Abortion

Few ethical issues are as bitterly fought over today as abortion, and, while the pendulum has swung back and forth, neither side has had much success in altering the opinions of its opponents. Until 1967, abortion was illegal in almost all the western democracies except Sweden and Denmark. Then Britain changed its law to allow abortion on broad social grounds, and in the 1973 case of *Roe v Wade*, the United States Supreme Court held that women have a constitutional right to an abortion in the first six months of pregnancy. Western European nations, including Roman Catholic countries like Italy, Spain and France, all liberalised their abortion laws. Only the Republic of Ireland held out against the trend.

Opponents of abortion did not give up... [T]he issue of abortion resurfaced in Eastern Europe after the collapse of communism. The communist states had allowed abortion, but as nationalist

You might decide to research these landmark rulings further before you move on in your reading or you might make a note to return to them.

What is the importance of reading that Catholic countries liberalised their approach to abortion?

and religious forces gathered strength, there were strong moves in countries like Poland for the reintroduction of restrictive laws. Since West Germany had more restrictive laws than East Germany, the need to introduce a single law for a united Germany also caused an intense debate.

You might need to brush up on your twentieth-century history to understand this paragraph fully and so might need to research further.

You might be interested in the context of Louise Brown or what current statistics are for IVF. You might pause to note down this example as a case study that you can use in your work.

In 1978 the birth of Louise Brown raised a new issue about the status of early human life. For Louise Brown was the first human to have been born from an embryo that had been fertilised outside a human body… IVF is now a routine procedure for certain types of infertility, and has given rise to thousands of healthy babies. To reach this point, however, many more embryos had to be destroyed in experiments, and further improvement of IVF techniques will require continued experimentation. Perhaps more significant still, for the long term, are the possibilities for other forms of experimentation opened up by the existence of a viable embryo outside the human body. Embryos can now be frozen and stored for many years before being thawed and implanted in a woman. Normal children develop from these embryos, but the technique means that there are large numbers of embryos now preserved in special freezers around the world. (At the time of writing there were about 11,000 frozen embryos in Australia alone.) Because the IVF procedure often produces more embryos than can safely be transferred to the uterus of the woman from whom the egg came, many of these frozen embryos will never be wanted, and presumably will either be destroyed, be donated for research, or given to other infertile couples.

You would need to be clear what the significance of talking about destroying embryos is for the abortion debate and the question of when life can be said to begin and whose right it is to destroy life.

You could pause here to find out how many frozen embryos are stored in the UK and what they are used for, especially remembering that the text is over 25 years old.

Intensive reading can develop strong skills to use in your exam. You could consider what different ethical theories would make of the idea of creating, storing, using and destroying embryos, for example — or what they would say about the rights of the woman from whom the egg came.

Other new technologies loom just a little way ahead. Embryos can be screened for genetic abnormalities, and then discarded if such

Who is Edwards? This particular book has a section of notes and references which point you towards an article Robert Edwards has written. Edwards also features in the index, so you can cross-reference what he says elsewhere. In other books, you might look at a bibliography at the end of the book to find out more.

How far has this scientific ability continued since the book was written?

> abnormalities are found. Edwards has predicted that it will become scientifically feasible to grow embryos in vitro to the point at which, about 17 days after fertilisation, they develop blood stem cells, which could be used to treat various now-lethal blood diseases. Others, speculating about the further future, have asked if one day we will have banks of embryos or fetuses to provide organs for those who need them.

Does this speculation still exist today?

From the passage, can you tell what direction the chapter is likely to go in? It goes through each of the points raised in this introduction in detail and surveys the views of key ethical points. Singer's views about the rights of a fetus are that it has the same status as any non-human animal with similar ability to reason. He extends this to newborn babies that themselves cannot reason and the rights of the newborn are determined not by anything intrinsic to the baby but by the wishes of those around them. If your views differ, would your introduction to the same chapter select different material? Your further reading might point you towards a very recent change in Singer's ethical stance, too, and you might consider the impact of his moving away from Preference Utilitarianism on this topic.

Extensive reading

Extensive reading will be used in your 'reading around' a topic, in the subject as a whole or simply in your reading for pleasure. It is used to gain an overall understanding of a text and you can then decide how you are going to take that reading further. In order to keep it active, it is useful to add anything that is subject-related to a notepad or a piece of paper in your general notes, simply to keep track of what you are reading. If you find a text uninteresting or difficult, you might persevere a bit but you might also not complete the book or article.

Activity

Go to the BBC News homepage (www.bbc.co.uk/news) and scroll down to the selection of articles called 'Long Reads'. Pick one or two articles and read them to try to get a sense of the story. Then, try to explain what you have read to someone else.

Reading goals

As you read, you should try to remain detached from the text. Just as moral objectivism in the ethics course tells us, there are moral truths that are completely separate to what an individual thinks or feels is right or wrong (subjectivism), so too being objective means that you detach yourself from your feelings about the text in order to understand it fully.

Know your goal

As we have seen, reading has the best outcomes when you are clear what your goal is. Apart from those considered above, you might also want to explore some of these other goals from time to time:

→ **Being inspired** — read in order to work out your solution to an issue or to be inspired about your long-term goals in the subject. Is this the right subject for you at university?

→ **Gaining general knowledge** — reading is, of course, one of the best ways to improve your general knowledge. Don't be afraid to read simple books that give you an overview about something you do not know. For example, when studying Bonhoeffer, you might find you want to learn more of the basics about Hitler and the Nazi Party and you might choose to start with a GCSE history textbook.

→ **Improving your vocabulary** — academic texts will, of course, help you to use theological and philosophical terms with greater accuracy. This type of reading may take time as you stop to understand words or look them up.

→ **Improving your written communication** — spelling, punctuation and grammar, as well as overall written communication, can be learned best through reading, not just through being corrected when you get it wrong in an essay.

→ **Destressing** — reading is a classic form of relaxation. Always have a novel in a genre you enjoy to hand.

→ **Passing on the tradition** — by choosing A-level religious studies, you will have chosen to step into the tradition of thousands of years of writers. Learn from the masters and be part of a long line of thinkers.

Bias

Texts are often full of bias. Hopefully, your textbooks and other learning resources won't be, but you will certainly encounter websites, articles and books that are written from a faith standpoint. Remaining objective will ensure that you can read through this and can ask yourself particular questions as you read, for example:

→ What is the author trying to achieve?

→ Are they using sources objectively? How else could the sources be interpreted?

→ Is the information going to be useful for my course?

→ Are the views scholarly views or are they the views of a blogger?

→ Does this contradict what I have learned in class?

The last question is really important. If, while you are reading, you find material that completely contradicts what you have covered in class, then you need to ask yourself why. It is important to check with your teacher or to confirm the different information from a second, reliable source.

Resilience

As you are reading, you will often encounter things that just seem too difficult, especially at the start. Struggle on! You will get used to it and the benefits will be obvious over time. Academic writing often has long sentences because the writers are aiming for absolute precision — especially in philosophy. If you are really struggling, it might be worth going back a step to get a little more background on the topic. Alternatively, ask your teacher to help you with a text: sometimes they can give you a way through it just by explaining a certain part. However, sometimes you will just need to put the time in: writing out a difficult paragraph in your own words or re-reading a section several times with a dictionary to hand. The moment when the meaning clicks is a massive reward.

Activity

Identify some words, phrases and styles used in a piece of academic writing. Think about the overall style as much as individual words. Then take the last essay you wrote and rewrite a paragraph in a more academic style.

Note-taking when reading

Many of the tips in Chapter 1 about note-taking in class are relevant here. When note-taking in your reading, you will often be trying to add to your class notes. Sometimes, you might make notes from a book to sit alongside your class notes that can then be brought together into your end-of-topic notes. You might also have a piece of paper to jot down things that are interesting but not relevant to your current goal. These can go into a file for another day, rather than for your exam preparation.

You will probably want to have two key things in your mind when you are taking notes from books: whether it is relevant material and whether it is new to you. This will help you to decide what is important. Look out for:

→ new scholars who can enhance your material on a topic

→ new arguments, strengths and weaknesses

→ new quotations

→ different ways of approaching a topic or defining a word

→ key concepts or big questions

You never want to be writing everything down. Be selective in what notes you take. At the same time, you don't want to be looking up the resource again, so make sure that there is sufficient detail to get everything clear for you to return to, perhaps in 18 months' time.

! Common pitfall

Never simply write out everything from any resource. This is passive, not active, note-taking. Write things in your own words and engage with the material. If you disagree with something, include that in your notes, too.

Bibliographies

Bibliographies are relevant in two ways. First, they are there as a guide to the key materials that someone has used to prepare a text or write a book. Second, they are there for you to use to further your reading, so enjoy dipping in to the different resources suggested. In particular, those bibliographies at the end of chapters in your textbook or articles written for A-level students will be designed to stretch you appropriately.

You also need to create your own bibliography. When you are writing notes from a book or an article, it is good practice to write the details of the resource at the top of your notes. When using websites, make sure you note the date you accessed the site and when using books, the relevant page numbers, especially if you ever quote directly from a book. You can also keep a detailed bibliography sheet for each topic along with your notes for that topic.

Take it further

Find an online guide on how to write bibliographies and begin using it immediately. The University of Leicester has an excellent guide at: www2.le.ac.uk/offices/ld/resources/writing/writing-resources/ref-bib

Reading set texts

All exam boards require you to know set passages for the study of your chosen religion. In addition, Edexcel requires you to study certain set texts from its anthology so that you can write essays responding to an extract in the exam. The skills discussed in this section will be relevant to other boards, too, if you are exposed to the writings of scholars in class.

Scripture passages

It is important that you have studied scripture passages sufficiently to be able to write a whole essay on any given passage. You will cover the scriptures in detail in class but outside of class it is useful to apply your reading skills to these passages. The annotated example below shows you how.

✓ Exam tip

The scripture in the annotated example is included in the AQA specification for Christianity. It is also the final 11 verses of a longer passage included in the OCR specification. Those studying for other exam boards are likely to have encountered the Sermon on the Mount and the techniques described are applicable to all scripture passages, whether from Christianity or not.

☰ Annotated example 2.3

Matthew 5:38–48
(New International Version)

You have heard that it was said, 'Eye for eye, and tooth for tooth.' But I tell you, do not resist an evil person. If anyone slaps you on the right cheek, turn to them the other cheek also. And if anyone wants to sue you and take your shirt, hand over your coat as well. If anyone forces you to go one mile, go with them two miles. Give to the one who asks you, and do not turn away from the one who wants to borrow from you.

You have heard that it was said, 'Love your neighbour and hate your enemy.' But I tell you, love your enemies and pray for those who persecute you, that you may be children of your

Intensive reading would make you stop to wonder where this was said. It is an Old Testament saying that Jesus is updating in this passage.

Skimming would tell you that this is a device that Jesus is using. You could consider (for AO2) whether it is a technique of the historical Jesus or whether it is Matthew imposing an author's style.

Scanning would help you find this key quotation (or a different one) to learn.

Analysis of this paragraph (AO2) shows that Jesus is tightening up the Old Testament approach. Some say that Jesus was replacing the Law, and this leads into useful evaluation in an essay.

Intensive reading would ensure that you understand the significance of Jesus mentioning 'tax collectors', 'your own people' and 'pagans'. If not, you would stop and research them.

Father in heaven. He causes his sun to rise on the evil and the good and sends rain on the righteous and the unrighteous.

If you love those who love you, what reward will you get? Are not even the tax collectors doing that?

And if you greet only your own people, what are you doing more than others? Do not even pagans do that ? Be perfect, therefore, as your heavenly Father is perfect.

Here you can **make links** to your study of the afterlife. It seems people have to work harder to be saved. The final sentence implies heaven and hell. An essay on the passage could include critical analysis of ideas of salvation and the afterlife.

You could **create** a symbol or image to help you remember this key point and Jesus' teachings in the passage.

Anthology texts

After you have studied the anthology texts, you should be in a position to comment on the passage that is set in the exam and use the text as a way in to answering the questions that follow. In your notes, how you read the texts will determine how prepared you are for whichever passage you get.

As you annotate the extracts, keep the following tips in mind and perhaps annotate them using a series of colours.

→ Use **skimming** to get a sense of the whole extract. You might look for particular topics covered in the extract but don't forget any general topic areas that are also touched on. For example, Barclay on situation ethics might well lead to consideration of other ethical theories. Make a note of these big topic areas to look out for at the top of the extract.

→ Use **scanning** to identify where in the extract the key words that are related to these topics might appear.

→ Ensure you can **link** the whole of a topic area to the sections in the extract. For example, what would you write about other aspects of falsification, given an extract from the 'Theology and Falsification' symposium?

→ For each paragraph or section, **analyse** the contentious issues that come out of just that section of text. Imagine it was your extract — what might you be asked to write about?

The extract in the exam

When faced with the extract in the exam it is important to read it carefully and efficiently. Training yourself to do this in advance will maximise your chances. Read it three times:

→ First, to make sure you know where it comes from in the anthology text.

→ Second, to highlight the key concepts and issues that are raised.

→ Third, after reading the two questions that follow, to be clear how you will refer to the passage in your answer.

✓ **Exam tip**

This section applies mainly to Edexcel, but it is helpful if you are reading the work of scholars in other situations.

! Common pitfall

Don't let yourself down by not re-reading the extract in the exam and simply rushing to answer the question. Treat the passage as if it is fresh and annotate it carefully.

Annotated example 2.4

You can see here that with some very simple annotation, you can bring out the key words that can then be used in your answer and lead you into analysis and evaluation (AO2).

Passage comes after Kant (in *Groundwork for the Metaphysics of Morals*) explains hypothetical and categorical imperatives.

Categorical imperative — not grounded on any other aim. Not to do with the action or its results but with its principle.

Hypothetical and categorical imperatives

If I think of a *hypothetical* imperative in general, then I do not know beforehand what it will contain until the condition is given to me. But if I think of a *categorical* imperative, then I know directly what it contains. For since besides the law, the imperative contains only the necessity of the maxim, that it should accord with this law, but the law contains no condition to which it is limited, there remains nothing left over with which the maxim of the action is to be in accord, and this accordance alone is what the imperative really represents necessarily. The categorical imperative is thus only a single one, and specifically this: Act only in accordance with that maxim through which you can at the same time will that it become a universal law.

Imperative — an ought — that gains something if you will it.

Law not contingent on anything (does morality *have* to be like this?.

Necessity is key.

Hypothetical imperative does contain condition.

Hypothetical imperative has something left over. Categorical imperative is unconditioned.

Needs to be a universal law of nature. Second formulation comes out of first, this is the key.

Passage goes on to explore universalisability. (Is universalisability realistic?)

You should know

> How good reading leads to good note-taking, which can lead to good results.
> That reading is essential to developing the key skills needed for writing.
> That good reading is always active, not passive.
> The goal(s) to have in mind when you are reading.
> The different reading skills to use — skimming, scanning, intensive or extensive.
> The set texts and how your reading skills can be used to enhance your understanding of them.
> How to enjoy reading as much for pleasure as you do for work.

3 Writing skills

Approaching different types of essays

This chapter takes you through some of the different things you need to remember when writing essays. In the exam, you are assessed entirely by extended writing and so it cannot be emphasised enough that the art of essay writing needs to be the one you practise the most over the 2-year course. Learn from your mistakes each time, especially by following the advice of your teacher, and aim to get better bit by bit so that you move yourself forwards throughout your course.

There are essentially three types of essay you will produce during your religious studies course: homework essays, timed essays and exam essays.

Homework essays

Homework essays are longer, giving you the opportunity to write more arguments for and against. They help you to learn the craft of essay writing and allow you to develop your voice as a religious studies student. They are the ideal time to experiment with different techniques, too. Sometimes your teacher will set you an essay that is more challenging than you might get in the exam or broader than time would allow for in the exam.

It is realistic to expect to spend 4 hours on a homework essay, including the preparation, or more if your interest is sparked. The time should be spent:

→ collecting together class notes
→ reviewing the textbook if necessary
→ doing further reading (see Chapter 2)
→ planning your essay
→ writing it

The key here is not to be writing the essay before you have decided that you have a real grasp of what you want to say.

> **! Common pitfall**
>
> Try not to box up your time too much — allow some time for inspiration to grab you. If your school or college allows for 6 hours of non-directed work a week, it is fine to do more if you love what you're doing. Just don't overdo it.

Timed essays

Your teacher will set you test essays in class and give you the same amount of time as you would get in the exam. These tests are really valuable, however annoying they may seem at the time. You are not likely to have your notes with you and you will begin to feel the pressure a bit, which is good practice. It is unlikely you will know the title in advance.

Again, you should expect to spend 4–5 hours preparing for one of these essays:

→ Collect together your class notes.
→ Make notes from the textbook.
→ Do further reading around the topic.
→ Learn the material carefully (see Chapter 4 for ideas about strategies).
→ Predict some possible questions and write essay plans.

Then, when you are under the test conditions, plan your essay (see below) and write it.

Exam essays

While these are a bit like timed essays, they differ in two key senses, whether they are for the final exam or for a mock exam:

→ You are going to write more than one essay, back to back.
→ You won't know which topics are coming up.

Revision for the exams is covered in Chapter 4 but one really useful tip is to choose all your questions (if you have a choice, depending on the exam board) at the start of the exam and to plan them all at the start. Then, write your strongest essay first, being disciplined with time. This means that if you think of something else to put in one of the other essays while you are writing, you will be able to amend your plan quickly.

Activity

Create your own exam paper and pick the topics you would dread coming up. After a few months, come back to the paper to see if you feel more confident and reflect on how you can ensure there are no surprises in the final exam.

Deconstructing the questions

Command words

A question is made up of command (or trigger) words or phrases plus the subject-specific content. It is important to be clear about what different command words will require of you. Table 3.1 gives examples.

Table 3.1 Command words used in A-level religious studies questions

Command word	Description
Analyse	Analyse a view or an argument to explore whether it is coherent. Reach a judgement about whether it is important or correct or relevant.
(Critically) Assess	Take the view that is offered and explore its strengths and weaknesses, reaching a judgement about whether it is correct or not.
Clarify	Explain the key concepts and ideas. Used as an AO1 command word by some exam boards.
(Critically) Compare	Explore the strengths and weaknesses of two aspects of a topic and reach a judgement about whether one or other provides a solution (or neither does). Do the strengths of one overcome the weaknesses of the other?
(Critically) Discuss	Explore the topic presented, analysing strengths and weaknesses or a specific view to reach a judgement.
(Critically) Evaluate	Analyse information and explore strengths and weaknesses to reach a judgement.
Examine	Give a detailed explanation of a topic or argument. Used as an AO1 command word by some exam boards.
Explain	Give a detailed explanation of a topic or argument or the views of a scholar, showing understanding. Used as an AO1 command word by some exam boards.
Explore	Explore different aspects of a topic or theme and reach a judgement about the strengths and weaknesses of it.
To what extent	Explore the statement offered by analysing strengths and weaknesses and reach your own judgement. The issue in this type of question is often less clear cut and there might be a middle ground that needs to be explored. You might fully agree or disagree but equally, you might agree with some aspects of the issue.
(A statement followed by) Discuss or Evaluate this claim	In this form of question, you need to evaluate the statement by picking arguments for and against it and show your own judgement about it.

You will see that you don't have to worry about the word 'critically' in a question because all it is doing is reminding you to do what makes a good essay anyway: to analyse and evaluate.

However, it is clear that most essay command words (apart from the AO1 ones used by some exam boards) require you to do the same thing: explore a topic, argument or scholar's views, showing that you understand them, have a view on them and have considered their strengths and weaknesses in reaching your view. In the exam, you are likely to have considered all this before and have your own views on the whole course, and you will certainly have the skills to think on your feet if necessary.

BUG the question

When faced with the question you are going to answer, the next thing to do is to deconstruct it carefully. It is important to take a few seconds to do this so that you do not go down the wrong path. More than anything else, you must answer the exact question on the paper in front of you.

One technique to help you do this is the 'BUG' technique (Figure 3.1):

→ **Box** — put a box around the command word.

→ **Underline** — underline the words in the question that give the question its particular focus.

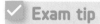

Exam tip

The examiner will not be trying to catch you out — ever! If you cannot quite see the point to a question, sadly you have to assume the issue is at your end. Either pick a different question or (if you have no choice) look at another question and then come back to the difficult one.

Common pitfall

You may simply see a topic or scholar mentioned in a question and begin to write about it, while not focusing on the actual question that has been set. This will lead to low marks, however good the information and analysis in your answer.

→ **Glance** — re-read the question to ensure that you haven't missed anything. Your mind will be whirring by now with ideas for you to put into your plan so it is an important check that you are doing the right thing.

Example 1

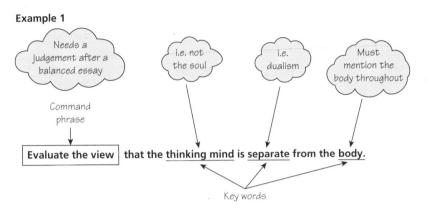

Example 2

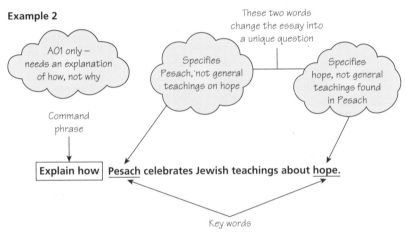

Figure 3.1 Examples of the BUG technique

Preparing to respond

Once you know the direction of the question you are going to answer, you are in a position to start to craft your essay. But, like a good piece of artwork, you need to sketch it out first with a plan.

Line of argument

And before you can plan, you need to know what you are going to be saying in the essay. Before you start to write, you need to be clear what your judgement is going to be — what are you going to conclude? Are you going to be supporting a particular scholarly approach or agreeing with the statement in the question? As you then move on to plan your essay, you can show why arguments for your view are useful and why arguments against your view are not relevant or can be discounted. It will also make you sound authoritative in the essay, which is an important tone to set.

A solid line of argument from the outset ensures consistency throughout the essay (see Table 3.2). We shall see later on how this can be written into the introduction. A good line of argument can be expressed in a single, straightforward sentence — and it certainly must answer the question!

If you imagine a topic as a painting, an essay simply asks you to look at a specific part of that painting. Imagine yourself peering at a small section of a painting. Establishing your line of argument allows you to step back and remember the painting as a whole.

Table 3.2 Possible lines of argument

Topic	Essay question	Possible line of argument	Comment
Body and soul (philosophy)	Evaluate the view that the thinking mind is separate from the body.	All of a person's identity comes from the physical.	Whatever the phrasing of the question, this student does not agree that there is a separate thinking mind and so this will guide their essay towards rejecting the view being evaluated.
Ontological Argument (philosophy)	To what extent is the Ontological Argument successful in proving the existence of God?	A priori arguments do not work in proving God's existence.	Given the student's approach, the Ontological Argument (as an a priori argument) will be said to be unsuccessful.
Free will (ethics)	'Philosophical, scientific and psychological evidence clearly supports libertarianism.' Evaluate this view.	All things are predetermined by God.	The student will be arguing against the statement through the essay. This line of argument is a good example of having a view about the topic as a whole that is applied to the specific question.
Knowledge of God (Christianity)	'Religious experience gives Christians knowledge of God.' Discuss.	Religious experiences can be understood psychologically and do not link to God.	This student will reject the statement on the basis that religious experiences can be explained by psychology rather than by God.

Activity

Find some essay titles and practise stating your line of argument on a single, tiny sticky note. If you struggle to condense it, think through the aspects of the question carefully before trying again.

The essay plan

There are two extremes when planning essays, both of which are a mistake. You can make it up as you go along, or you can write out most of your essay in the plan. If you do the first, you will find yourself not being clear about your line of argument and ending up missing out important information — or wishing you had saved an argument for a different paragraph. If you do the second, you will waste time and energy which could be better channelled into the essay itself.

A01 and A02 essays

The best plans are those that focus on the question and your line of argument. Rather than simply writing out what you know on a topic, you focus on the points for and against the statement or question. There is no need to write out the A01 points in detail because they should be safely stored in your mind (in an exam) or in your notes (for a homework essay).

! Common pitfall

In your plan, don't put all the best information at the start of the essay. This isn't useful because it means that your reader will get to the end of the essay and think you have lost steam. It is better to plan in advance where you are going to say what and how you are going to group certain arguments and counter-arguments.

Once you have worked out your line of argument, you need to jot down the relevant number of main points for and against the statement or issue. Each of these main points is a major paragraph. Within this paragraph will come a mixture of AO1 points and other AO2 discussion points.

After you have done this, you can add in prompts to yourself to ensure that you cover all the relevant information over the course of your essay. A sample essay plan is shown in the example below, with the prompts highlighted in different colours.

> **✓ Exam tip**
>
> Look at the final section of this book for details about your particular exam board's requirements. The length of time you have for an essay will, of course, determine how many major paragraphs there are in your essay, but 7–8 minutes per major paragraph is a good estimation.

Annotated example 3.1

Evaluate the view that the thinking mind is separate from the body.

LOA = line of argument. The essay would have an introduction (and a conclusion) but as this is obvious, it doesn't need spelling out in the plan.

The case studies do not need to be written out because they have been learned.

Plan

LOA: all a person's identity comes from the physical

Thinking mind is separate from the body	Thinking mind is not separate from the body
Personalities etc. do not depend on whether we lose a leg. Case studies from class/medical evidence — complexities of medical knowledge.	Evidence from DNA shows that everything is interconnected. Dawkins and the role of science — discuss Dawkins.
Thought is a purer aspect than things that come from the body. Plato & Descartes Issues with both.	There is no evidence for the separation of substances. Ryle — weak philosophy.

Carefully including the wording of the question ensures focus throughout the answer.

AO2 points are included in the plan throughout. It is likely that the discussion about Dawkins would be favourable because of the LOA, but balance would still be needed.

The danger here is that the student writes for too long about Plato and Descartes. They could focus their mind by writing 'Plato: Forms' or 'Descartes: cogito'.

Again, no detail is needed here because the student has stored in their mind the relevance of 'there is no evidence' being weak philosophy.

The difference between...

A key difference between weaker and stronger plans (and therefore essays) is the extent to which they are **argument-driven**. Look at how the B-grade essay plan below focuses on AO1 knowledge rather than AO2 arguments. It would be easy for the student to end up writing out everything they know about a scholar rather than making the essay AO2-focused (and they would be lucky to get a B in that case).

B grade	A* grade
• Case studies about what happens when someone loses a leg. • Plato/Descartes. • Dawkins. • Ryle.	• Personalities etc. do not depend on whether we lose a leg. • Thought is a purer aspect than things that come from the body. • Evidence from DNA shows that everything is interconnected. • There is no evidence for the separation of substances.

A01-only essays

Where your writing requires only A01 knowledge and understanding, your plan should be very brief indeed and is likely to be a quick series of bullet points. You only need to write down the key points to ensure that you cover everything in the time available, as shown in the example below.

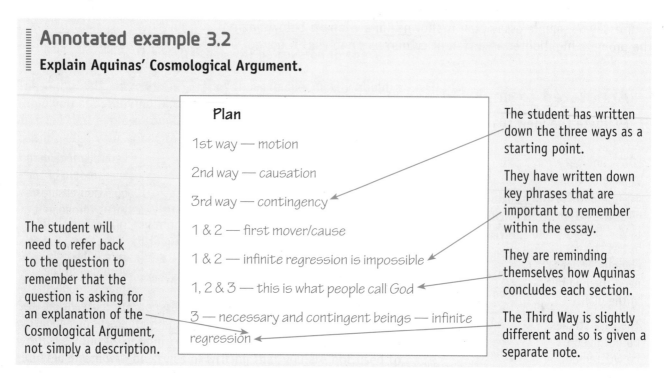

Annotated example 3.2

Explain Aquinas' Cosmological Argument.

The student will need to refer back to the question to remember that the question is asking for an explanation of the Cosmological Argument, not simply a description.

> **Plan**
>
> 1st way — motion
>
> 2nd way — causation
>
> 3rd way — contingency
>
> 1 & 2 — first mover/cause
>
> 1 & 2 — infinite regression is impossible
>
> 1, 2 & 3 — this is what people call God
>
> 3 — necessary and contingent beings — infinite regression

The student has written down the three ways as a starting point.

They have written down key phrases that are important to remember within the essay.

They are reminding themselves how Aquinas concludes each section.

The Third Way is slightly different and so is given a separate note.

A02-only essays

There is a sense in which A02-only essays are a myth. If your exam board has split A01/A02 questions, then you need to be clear that the A02 part is wishing you to arrive at a judgement by analysing evidence. If the first (A01) part of the question was linked, then some of your work has been done for you, but this is not always the case. In these questions, you should plan as above but when you come to write, you need to ensure that your phrasing shows you are in control of the information and could write more if you had been asked to. For example:

→ Plato's Theory of Forms illustrates this idea of reality not being in this world (i.e. not writing out Plato's full theory)

→ ...as seen in Bentham's focus on individual events as opposed to Mill's more rule-based approach... (i.e. not explaining Bentham and Mill in detail: it is obvious you know them both)

→ ...as illustrated by the common criticism of Mahayana that there is too much focus on nibbana... (i.e. you do not need to write out the differences between different Buddhist schools of thought)

Writing the essay
The introduction

Introductions are often the most overthought part of an essay. On their own they gain no marks but without one an essay can seem incomplete to an examiner. The worst introductions:

→ express confusion from the outset (e.g. describing theologians as philosophers)

→ simply restate the question in different (or even the same) words

→ use sweeping generalisations

→ use pointless phrases (e.g. 'this has been an issue for many years')

→ show ignorance about the bigger picture (e.g. 'this topic was discussed first by Aquinas and then by Copleston' — no, these are just the two people listed on the specification)

 Exam tip

An introduction is only needed for a unified (AO1+AO2) essay. Other essays do not give you the time for an introduction, although sometimes they could benefit from an opening sentence using the same techniques described in this section.

Activity

Examine each of the introductions below and decide how you would improve them. Then return to this activity after you have read this section to see if you could improve them further.

Essay question	Introduction
Evaluate the view that the thinking mind is separate from the body.	This is from the topic of the mind and the body. Some scholars say that the thinking mind is separate from the body and others reject this view because they say the thinking mind is a part of the body. I disagree.
To what extent is the Ontological Argument successful in proving the existence of God?	For many years, scholars have explored the idea of the Ontological Argument. Anselm and Descartes are known proponents of the argument and Gaunilo and Kant reject it because its logic is weak. We shall see that their argument is weak because a priori arguments can never prove the existence of God.
'Philosophical, scientific and psychological evidence clearly supports libertarianism.' Evaluate this view.	In this essay I am going to explore the view that philosophical, scientific and psychological evidence clearly supports libertarianism. I will evaluate different approaches from scholars and come to a conclusion.
'Religious experience gives Christians knowledge of God.' Discuss.	The nature of religious experience is that it is by definition personal and unverifiable. Christians would argue that it is one of the best ways of knowing God because it is a form of direct revelation; however, some psychologists would reject this view on the basis that religious experience can be explained in other ways. I think that religious experiences are not genuine for this reason.

The point of an introduction

An introduction serves to engage your reader from the outset and to help them decide if they are going to bother to read your essay. Remember in the chapter on reading skills, we saw that good skimming often includes reading the introduction.

A good introduction will:

→ show that you understand the question

→ show that you understand the bigger picture (i.e. why this essay question is such an important topic that it made it onto an A-level course)

→ state your line of argument

→ give a sense of how you are going to approach the question

If you can express all this very concisely, you will persuade the examiner that your script is going to be worth their effort and that they should look favourably on you when awarding marks.

Writing a great introduction

An introduction should be proportionate to the length of your essay, which could mean:

→ 10% of the total time
→ half of the size of a major paragraph
→ no more than a quarter of a side of writing (depending on your handwriting size)
→ the same length as the conclusion

One way to turn your introduction into a great one is to follow the CBA technique to turn your C into an A: **c**ontext, **b**rains, **a**pproach.

Context

The 'context' part of the introduction is your opening sentence or two. You need to make it count. You are likely to:

→ define the bounds of the question
→ define any core concepts
→ show you are clear about the bigger picture

Annotated example 3.3

'Religious experience gives Christians knowledge of God.' Discuss.

Sweeping generalisation which doesn't tell the examiner anything useful.

Weak start

For thousands of years people have claimed to have had religious experiences and some believe them and others do not.

Vague: no development.

Apart from essentially restating the idea of 'discuss' this sentence shows that the student has not focused on the question sufficiently and has not noticed that the question links religious experience to knowledge of God.

Stronger start

With the overwhelming number of claimed religious experiences and types of religious experience even within Christianity, it is necessary to explore the extent to which they are genuine revelations, for, if they are, they can, by definition, give knowledge of God.

Authoritative phrase that expresses control over the content.

Uses the wording of the question to keep focused.

Useful differentiation between quantity and category, which acts as a definition of the topic of religious experience.

Shows an understanding of the context and defines the phrase 'knowledge of God'.

Brains

The 'brains' part of the introduction allows you to state which key scholars, scholarly viewpoints or case studies will be used in the essay. This part should not read like a shopping list but should show that the essay has been well crafted and thought through.

Annotated example 3.4

Here are two good examples of the brains part of an introduction. Both assume a preceding sentence or two for the context part of the introduction.

'Equality of gender is an impossible ideal within Sikhism.' Discuss.

A clear, authoritative tone is adopted.

> We shall explore the contrast between Sikh communities in the West and those in the Punjab and the implications of the girl as paraya dhan and the growing leadership role women play in Sikhism.

A clear statement that two viewpoints or scholarly views will be explored rather than just listing scholars for the sake of it.

'Philosophical, scientific and psychological evidence clearly supports libertarianism.' Evaluate this view.

> This essay will explore the wealth of evidence in favour of libertarianism, such as that from Sartre and modern scientific developments, and contrast it with the views of Locke and Skinner to explore the extent to which free will is simply an illusion.

More specific scholars are mentioned in this example but the student is successfully mixing in wider views to demonstrate that they realise that a view can be held by many scholars at once.

Approach

In this part of your introduction, you need to make sure your line of argument is clear in a concise and interesting way. You can even join it on to the previous part in a flowing sentence, for example:

→ By contrasting the views of Bradley and Moore, it will become clear that meta ethics requires a factual basis...

This is the point at which your essay can clearly be seen to be an act of persuading your reader to join you in your viewpoint. This is not a conclusion, however, and you haven't yet presented your argument in full, so your comments should remain relatively simple.

The example below demonstrates that the CBA technique can be personalised as much as desired. Of course, none of the good introductions you have seen here could have been achieved without a good and effective essay plan.

Activity

Go back over some recent essays and improve your introductions using the CBA technique. Try to find your own style and approach and don't be too formulaic — remember your examiner could be reading up to four of your essays in a row.

Annotated example 3.5

To what extent is the Ontological Argument successful in proving the existence of God?

Due to careful planning, the student knows that the a priori approach will be central to their essay and so ensures it is present in the introduction.

A gentle but authoritative presentation of the student's line of argument.

> The Ontological Argument, put forward by Anselm as a prayer and Descartes independently several hundred years later, uses an a priori approach to try to prove God's existence, thus differing from many other arguments. We shall see that Anselm's argument, while not defeated by Gaunilo, is weak simply as an a priori argument and that, as demonstrated by Kant, such arguments can never prove God's existence.

The student shows context, a timeline and the key scholars in favour of the Ontological Argument.

Shows the bigger picture: the Ontological Argument versus other arguments.

Introduces the scholars against the argument.

You can see how concisely the introduction has been written — anything more would lose the attention of the reader.

AO1-only essays

If your exam board has two-part questions, the first part will be an AO1-only essay. Not all of your essays will be AO1-only essays so make sure you are clear which is which — use the information on command words (pp. 31–32) and the final section on exam board requirements to help you.

As we saw in the introduction, some of the things we are trying to do here to gain high marks are:

→ to include a wide range of material
→ to select material that is comprehensively and clearly developed
→ to make your essay thorough, accurate, relevant and extensive
→ to relate your essay to textual and scriptural references where necessary

Paragraph structure

The best way to achieve a good paragraph structure is to include an appropriate number of PEEL paragraphs, which is the most commonly used AO1 structure. PEEL stands for: **p**oint, **e**vidence, **e**xplanation, **l**ink.

Point

The idea of an AO1-only essay is not to write out the basics of a topic but to show a detailed understanding of it (in the time available) and you can begin this in the opening sentence. In your plan you will have identified an appropriate number of main paragraphs for your response. Each of these is a point.

Exam tip

This section is **not** relevant to OCR students.

Activity

Using the feedback from your last three or four pieces of AO1-only writing, identify which of the areas listed above are your strengths and which are areas you need to improve.

The difference between...

A general point	A focused point
Aquinas' first way starts with the idea of motion.	Aquinas believes God, a prime mover, exists because of the observation of motion.
Some Christians reject the idea of divorce.	Differences in attitudes to divorce often reflect the extent to which marriage is seen as sacramental.

Evidence

It is important to use just the right amount of material to illustrate your point and back it up. Practising your PEEL paragraphs during the 2-year course will ensure you can do this automatically. For evidence, you are deploying your knowledge and source references to answer the question. If you are answering a question on an extract for Edexcel, you will be quoting from the extract directly.

Explanation

This is where the majority of marks will be picked up as you move your response up through the levels. You need to give a tight explanation of how the evidence is relevant or relates to the question or what the scholar is trying to achieve. This is where your own voice comes through, not by reaching a judgement (that's AO2) but where you show you *own* the material yourself and you are in control.

Link

A link is a short sentence (or even a half-sentence joined on to the explanation section) that nods back to the question. It rounds off the paragraph and ensures that as you explore a topic you are still linking it back to the specific question.

> **! Common pitfall**
>
> Don't spend too long simply writing out the evidence for an argument and thereby lose sight of what you are trying to achieve in a PEEL paragraph. Move on from the evidence to the explanation as quickly as you can.

Annotated example 3.6

A PEEL paragraph in an AO1-only essay.

Explain how Pesach celebrates Jewish teachings about hope.

> During the Seder meal, the symbolism demonstrates elements of hope; for example, in dipping the parsley into the salt water (or vinegar) to taste the hope of rebirth alongside the tears and bitterness of slavery. This hope is drawn out through the years of history and the experience of the Jewish people and is a reminder of the historical message that G-d is always with them and will not ever leave them, even in times of need, a reminder of hope that is re-enacted in a particular way at each celebration of Pesach.

Point — the point of this paragraph is to explore symbolism at the Seder meal, which is an element of Pesach.

Evidence — the evidence used here is stated efficiently.

Link — the paragraph concludes by joining together the explanation with a link to the core elements of the question — Pesach and hope.

Explanation — the explanation broadens the context.

AO2-only and unified essays

AO2 essays are bread and butter for religious studies students. The best A-level exam essays show that you have engaged fully with the course over the 2 years and have become a theologian or philosopher in your own right. Success at this level requires:

→ a confident and authoritative style with precise subject vocabulary

→ perceptive discussion and insightful critical analysis of scholars or scholarly views

→ thorough and sustained writing that explores the question in full

→ a reasoned judgement that is well-justified

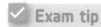 **Exam tip**

This section applies to all exam boards. It covers any essay with AO2 in it. Some exam boards have two-part questions where the second part focuses on AO2, but the essay structure needs to remain the same.

Paragraph structure

Examiners' reports are full of the need for AO1 and AO2 writing to be drawn together in a naturally flowing essay. The PACE paragraph structure helps you to get the balance right and should be applied to the series of major paragraphs you identified in your essay plan. For each of the key points for and against (four to six, depending on the length of your essay), you need to apply the PACE structure: **P**oint, **A**nalyse, **C**riticise, **E**valuate.

The difference between...

Satisfactory essays	Great essays
AO1 points are stated before the AO2 points.	AO1 and AO2 points are fully integrated.
The AO2 point is simply stated as being either for or against the issue.	AO2 points are developed, engaged with and expanded upon.
AO1 points dominate the essay and the essay gets stuck when the AO1 points run out.	The AO2 points control the selection of AO1 points.
Views are not fully justified.	All views are fully justified.
The question is not the focus of the essay.	The question guides the selection of material.
Arguments do not drive the essay forwards.	The essay is argument-driven.
The examiner always feels they want more.	The examiner is swept along by the authoritative writing style.

Point

This is one of the arguments for or against the issue that has come out of your planning. Basing your paragraphs around your identified points ensures that your entire essay is argument-driven and not information-driven. In order to illustrate this structure, the example below uses a general question.

Annotated example 3.7
'Burgers are better than pizzas.' Discuss.

The line of argument ensures consistency throughout the essay and allows you to plan what your judgement is going to be.

A suitable sentence starter.

This is a comparison question and so the arguments for and against need to reflect the comparison.

This is one of the major paragraph points that has been used to start a PACE paragraph.

Plan

LOA: pizzas are better on all levels — convenience, practicality, sophistication.

Burgers better than pizzas	Pizzas better than burgers
Burgers are more readily available in quicker time from fast-food outlets.	Pizzas come in a wider choice of varieties, including vegetarian.
Burgers are simpler to prepare than pizzas — bread can be bought easily ready-made, additional toppings can be grabbed at the last minute.	Pizzas are better because you can share one or have a smaller one to yourself. They are much more flexible.

Point for a PACE paragraph

A key argument for pizzas being better than burgers is the significantly greater range of possibilities and toppings available for pizzas, which means they are better at catering for many dietary needs.

There are a number of other sentence starters you can use in this context. You are essentially trying to come up with different ways of saying 'some people might (dis)agree with this because...'. In fact, many successful essays do use that phrase at the right time. Examples might be:

→ It seems that...
→ It could be said/argued that...
→ The statement could be rejected because...

Analyse

This is the part of the paragraph where you pick up the AO1 marks. If your essay is AO2-only (AQA, CCEA, Eduqas and WJEC), it is still important to include this section in order for the paragraph to make sense, but it will be significantly minimised. By analysis, we are trying to present some relevant information that is developed so that it fits the argument in the right place — it is like moulding a piece of playdough into a particular shape. The playdough is still the same piece, just developed in some way.

Exam tip

For synoptic essays (AQA, CCEA and Edexcel), this is the part of the paragraph where you make a direct link to one of your other papers as you unpack a concept. Board-specific points are covered in detail in the final section.

Annotated example 3.8
'Burgers are better than pizzas.' Discuss.

A key argument for pizzas being better than burgers is the significantly greater range of possibilities and toppings available for pizzas, which means they are better at catering for many dietary needs. While vegetarian burgers are available, there is no guarantee that the kitchen they have been prepared in separates meat from vegetarian frying pans. In a recent survey of pizza toppings at a well-known chain, just under half of the available toppings were vegetarian and there is always the opportunity to choose your own toppings. Gluten-free bases are also available.

The initial point.

A01 analysis is introduced which builds on the initial point.

The analysis is developed further with the use of appropriate knowledge and sources.

In some essays, this A01 analysis will involve explaining the relevant part of a key scholar's views — or even more than one. In others, you will be explaining an argument in detail or the relevant synoptic links. Here are some further examples.

Annotated example 3.9

Here is a summary of Hick's view which could equally be expanded with a relevant quotation. It ensures the student picks up A01 marks for showing they know what Hick said.

The analysis is taken further through the idea of lenses and the example of the blind men and the elephant. You can see the paragraph building up the point introduced in the P section.

	'Christianity is not the only means to salvation.' Discuss.	Evaluate the view that utilitarianism continues to offer a useful way of resolving moral dilemmas.
Point	Some might consider that Christianity is not the only means to salvation because religious experience is common to all faiths.	It might seem that the objectivity provided by utilitarianism is a less emotionally involved way of making moral decisions.
Analyse	Hick believed that all forms of worship in different religious traditions were valid ways of getting to God. He spoke of the differences between religions as simply being like different lenses through which we experience the same reality. The famous example is that of the blind men who each feel a different part of an elephant: it is still the same elephant, whichever angle they take, just as Hick suggests each religion is a different angle on reality.	Bentham's hedonic calculus treats all human life as having equal value and therefore ensures that there is complete separation from personal ties and decisions can be made purely according to the measure of pleasure and pain.

Again, this section on Bentham could be expanded or reduced, depending on the needs of the particular essay. The student could explain, with examples, the entirety of Bentham's hedonic calculus if this were the only major paragraph where they were planning to use Bentham in this essay.

You can see that mentions of the relevant scholars who made points or whose points you are using are saved until the second sentence in the paragraph. That way, your paragraph remains argument-driven and it forces you to focus on the higher-level AO2 skills rather than simply writing out theory.

Criticise

If you are out having a coffee with your friends and someone raises a point of discussion, the conversation would not stop the minute they had said their bit and then move on to a new topic. You would discuss the point in detail before moving on. In the same way, your essay needs to engage fully with the point you have raised at the beginning of a paragraph to examine the extent to which it is a valuable point and to show that your line of argument is still justified.

This part of a paragraph requires you to explore the strengths and weaknesses of the point you are in the middle of discussing. In the annotated example on the previous page, it would engage with Bentham's exclusion of family members from ethical decision making. If new information is needed, then it is introduced very quickly — for example, you might mention that a particular scholar agrees with the point being made but you would not give all the details of that scholar because you have chosen to give all the details of someone else. Remember that an essay is a *selection* of relevant material and never 'everything I ever learned'.

> ✅ **Exam tip**
>
> When you are planning your essay, you can ensure that you have included all the relevant AO1 points in the essay by picking in which paragraph to put different bits of information before you start writing.

> ❗ **Common pitfall**
>
> Don't make the criticise part all about the general strengths and weaknesses of the topic or the essay title. It is meant to be narrowed in on the paragraph you are writing. Each major paragraph can be thought of as a mini-essay.

Annotated example 3.10
'Burgers are better than pizzas.' Discuss.

A key argument for pizzas being better than burgers is the significantly greater range of possibilities and toppings available for pizzas, which means they are better at catering for many dietary needs. ← The initial point.

While vegetarian burgers are available, there is no guarantee that the kitchen they have been prepared in separates meat from vegetarian frying pans. In a recent survey of pizza toppings at a well-known chain, just under half of the available toppings were vegetarian and there is always the opportunity to choose your own toppings. Gluten-free bases are also available. ← Analysis of the point.

Criticism of the **point**, which can be positive or negative. → A strength of the argument in favour of pizzas is that there has been an increase in different dietary needs and more people are eating

New information is presented as concisely as possible.

vegetarian food (29% in 2018, compared with 27% in 2014). However, we have only been considering the burgers found in traditional, fast-food restaurants — there are other kinds of burger restaurants which might provide a greater range of options.

This criticism reduces the impact of the paragraph's focus on vegetarianism.

It is in this section of each paragraph that the requirements of the top level are really achieved because you are able to show thoroughness, depth, precision and critical analysis.

Evaluate

In this section of the major paragraph, you need to wrap up the mini-discussion you have been leading your reader through by drawing it back to the question. The best way to do this is to check the specific language of the question before you write. This ensures that you are focused precisely on what you are trying to achieve. You also need to ensure that the evaluation matches your line of argument.

It is acceptable to use the first person (I or we) in this sentence ('I think…' or 'We can see…') or a different style ('It is clear…', 'It seems evident…', 'Therefore…'). The best essays will use a mixture of phrases to avoid sounding too formulaic.

The difference between…

Unfocused evaluative sentence	Focused evaluative sentence
Therefore, overall, the idea of burgers still implies meat and bread and so they are bad for vegetarians.	Ultimately, although the range and availability of burgers are increasing, the focus is very much on meat and bread and so there is still more choice with pizzas, making pizzas preferable to burgers.

Once your paragraph is nicely rounded off, you can move on to the next PACE paragraph.

Activity

Take the last essay you did and rewrite a paragraph using the PACE structure. If you find you are being forced to develop the points you made, then it might be a good structure for you to adopt for all your essays.

Bringing the pieces together

The PACE structure begins when you identify the four to six key arguments for and against the issue in the question title that you are going to use.

These points become your major paragraphs. Each major paragraph follows the PACE structure and is a mini-discussion in itself.

If there is a lot to say then sometimes it is possible to break down a major paragraph into smaller, minor paragraphs — for example, you could start a new paragraph for the criticise part.

Annotated example 3.11

Critically assess Augustine's teaching on original sin.

The student has added prompts for themselves after deciding the points for and against. In doing this, they have decided where the A01 points are going to be mentioned so that all of Augustine's approach is covered.

As the essay is a 'critically assess' essay, the student has decided to explore the issue from the perspective of strengths and weaknesses.

LOA: unrealistic about human nature.

Strengths of Augustine's teaching	Weaknesses of Augustine's teaching
Makes sense of the Fall and why humans are prone to sin and are torn in different directions. Concupiscence/Romans 7.	Relies on a literal interpretation of Genesis which is not usually accepted. Pre/post-lapsarian: harmony vs shame.
Sexual desire is a central feature of the human experience, just like Augustine said. Lust/Freud.	All humans are tainted by the sin of two people, which seems unfair. Contracted, not committed (Catechism) Omnibenevolent God/did Jesus save?

PACE paragraph

The **p**oint is phrased confidently.

Some might suggest that Augustine's teaching on original sin should be rejected due to the requirement for the Fall story to be literally true. The Fall suggests that the first two humans, Adam and Eve, created as part of the Genesis creation story, were in a perfect relationship with God and each other and then, as a result of giving in to the temptation of the Devil, they broke this relationship. As a result, the post-lapsarian world went from harmony to shamefulness. The Genesis story can be rejected as literally true for two main internal reasons: that the Bible is full of contradictions, which suggests that it should not be taken literally, and also because there are clearly two different authors at work in Genesis who prepared the two creation stories as well as later chapters. Externally, the evidence of evolution points to a world which did not begin with just two humans, and surely there were early primates before humans who had sufficient reason to be able to sin. So it is possible to retain the story of the Fall with a more metaphorical understanding and it does not need to be literally taken as true. The Roman Catholic Church also sees the nature of original sin as a mystery, which would explain why it is difficult to understand. It seems, however, that these are insufficient reasons not to reject the Genesis story's truth and so potentially Augustine's entire reasoning about original sin.

The **a**nalysis introduces the key relationship and ties it in carefully to the argument of the paragraph. The student is careful not to go into too much narrative detail and shows that the story is completely understood in a minimal number of words.

The **e**valuation continues to be clear and coherent and maintains the line of argument as a judgement is reached and before the student goes on to the next major point.

The **c**riticism identifies both strengths and weaknesses of the idea of rejecting the Fall as literally true. Several points are covered swiftly and with precision — showing real thoroughness.

The conclusion

The conclusion is another part of the essay that many students let themselves down with because they do not fully appreciate its importance. A conclusion should not be rushed and it should not be an afterthought. It is the final touch to your carefully crafted piece of writing and you should enjoy writing it because you can bring together your powers of persuasion to get your point across once and for all.

Of course, the conclusion should not be a surprise. You will have made your line of argument clear from the outset and you will have indicated through your evaluative parts of each major paragraph what your interim judgements have been. The conclusion draws all this together and shows how these judgements have all been a part of the overall line of argument. If you are a mathematician or scientist, you will understand the function of a conclusion to be a straight line of best fit.

The conclusion is a firm but gentle statement for or against. You are an A-level student and so you still need to be respectful of viewpoints that you do not agree with. However, you do need to be confident in your judgement and in your evaluation of the common themes between the various points you have made. The conclusion needs to explain that judgement.

The conclusion should not:
→ begin with the words 'In conclusion' or 'Therefore'
→ restate each paragraph — that would be a summary
→ contradict your introduction
→ be rushed — make sure you have time to write it

Some possible conclusions for some of the essay questions in this section are given in the example below.

Exam tip

A conclusion is needed for AO2 essays only where a judgement is required. AO1 essays could end with a summary but this is unlikely to be necessary.

Annotated example 3.12

Possible conclusions to essay questions used previously.

'Burgers are better than pizzas.' Discuss.

A useful opening phrase for a conclusion which shows that this paragraph develops out of the previous ones.

We have seen that despite the simple accessibility of burgers, pizzas have readily adapted to the requirements of new dietary needs. There is a real sense of convenience to the pizza, despite the dough base, which just needs to be got used to. Although burgers are, in effect, sandwiches, pizzas do seem to have been shown to be better than burgers in most key areas.

A focused and precise return to the question.

Evaluate the view that the thinking mind is separate from the body.

It seems that the religious and philosophical approaches to the mind–body distinction all have significant flaws in them. Materialist approaches, such as that of Dawkins, acknowledge that not all questions have been fully understood but they allow for the answers to be forthcoming in the future. Although advances in science in this case seem to reject all religious viewpoints, a shift in understanding about the nature of reality might allow religion to continue to have a place in modern society. However, in this essay, the thinking mind seems to be part of or an aspect of bodily functions.

The opening phrase comes out of an essay that has clearly rejected the idea of a spiritual self throughout.

An acknowledgement that the conclusion comes out of a limited essay but shows the context for the conclusion.

To what extent is the Ontological Argument successful in proving the existence of God?

Although the essay is going to reject the Ontological Argument, it shows an openness to the other side.

Ultimately, the Ontological Argument's resurgence in recent years has opened the possibility to it successfully proving the existence of God. However, in no version does it successfully overcome the core challenge of how it attempts to use words to create an object — to define something into existence — and therefore it seems necessary to reject it as an argument for God's existence, perhaps in favour of a posteriori arguments.

This conclusion goes a bit wider to suggest what would essentially be the next step in research.

Critically assess Augustine's teachings on original sin.

Augustine's view of original sin and his approach to human nature by extension demonstrates a particular approach to viewing the world and human relationships which seems to have been replaced by modern understandings of humanity, relationships, libido and also the origins of people. However, Augustine's main fault, it seems to me, is to place all reasoning for humans being as they are in the hands of Adam and Eve at the Fall, which makes me reject his teaching on original sin and all that comes out of it.

Used carefully, the first person (me) is appropriate language to use in some conclusions.

General writing advice

Style

With all these tips and frameworks above, it is important to make sure that your style doesn't become too formulaic or robotic. The worst thing to read in an essay is a series of pre-learned phrases or sentence starters. There is only one way to avoid this: practise. You need to practise your PEEL or PACE structure so that you find different ways to transition between the different parts. Experiment with different words and phrases and see how your teacher takes to them when marking your work. Avoid words and phrases that do not really serve to help your essay or are unclear because they are too extreme, such as 'good/bad point', 'nice', 'thing' and 'passion' (these are also words I ban from my students' UCAS personal statements).

Table 3.3 has some useful words and phrases you might think about using — but develop your own, individual voice as much as possible.

Table 3.3 Useful words and phrases

Word or phrase	Useful because...
It is necessary/useful/important to	This academic style shows authority in your decision to use the following piece of information
For this reason...	Shows that you are clear about why you are selecting a particular piece of evidence
We shall explore four views...	Shows that in the limited time, you are clear what material you are selecting
X suggests/argues/claims/ demonstrates/shows/asserts	Shows you are clear about why a scholar makes a point — and avoids the word 'says'
Another/a further/furthermore	Shows that your point follows on logically from a previous one
Similarly/equally/consequently In addition	Further develops the points and can also be used inside a paragraph (don't forget to follow these with a comma)
However/whereas/nevertheless/ nonetheless/conversely/in contrast	Introduces a different point of view; useful in the criticise part of a PACE paragraph

Whichever words you choose to use in an essay, remember that you need to come across as:

→ clear
→ authoritative
→ precise
→ consistent
→ humble

And note that it is quality not quantity that counts. Each exam board uses different stationery, so it is difficult to talk about the 'right' amount to write in a certain amount of time, but remember, when you practise your essays, aim to improve the quality and not the quantity — be more thoughtful than hasty, 250 words in 10 minutes is *plenty*.

> **! Common pitfall**
>
> Sometimes you might learn words and phrases that are good in essays but then you don't use them with the precision they require — or you are not quite sure what a word means. It is better to write in your own style than use high-brow language that doesn't come naturally.

Take it further

Use a search engine to look up good phrases for essays or connectives for writing and make your own list of words and phrases to try out.

The basics

It is vital that you know the basics of your subject. You need to make sure that you come across well, but however authoritative your writing style is or your ability to compare two points of view, you will not endear yourself to your reader if you mess up the basics.

Jargon

Key words for the subject need to be properly deployed and not overused. One common mistake in essays is students using philosophical vocabulary inappropriately.

Activity

Take your textbook or revision guide and use the glossary at the back to test yourself on the key words for religious studies.

In addition to the technical terms that come through learning the subject there are some basic concepts that apply to religious studies. Make sure you are clear on:

→ the differences between a philosopher and a theologian

→ that fact that the Bible is a collection of books, each split into chapters and verses, each written at different times and often by different authors

→ the fact that not all members of a religion believe the same and that not all members of a denomination of any religion believe the same (but that in many religions there is official guidance or teaching with different levels of authority)

→ the names and titles of the leaders of the religions or denominations you will talk about in your essays

Timelines

The other embarrassing mistake that students can make is to show that they are unaware of the chronology of the subject. It is important not to suggest that Aristotle agreed with Hume and to realise that Plato came before Jesus, or that Hinduism is older than Sikhism. It is worth writing down the dates of the key people you study and making a timeline if it helps you. Getting this right will also help you to see areas of the subject or key debates in the appropriate context and will deepen your understanding even further.

Quotations

A common misconception is that taking time to learn and then regurgitate quotations from scholars is a guarantee of higher marks. This is a mistake because:

> **! Common pitfall**
>
> Learning by rote — that is, learning things out of context and word for word — is not the key to success. Just as you wouldn't use your notes or a book word for word, you shouldn't be using quotations word for word.

→ when you learn only a few quotations you feel you have to use them whatever happens in an essay — and therefore often misuse them

→ quotations need explaining and so you might as well have explained the scholar's view in more detail and omitted the quotation

→ sometimes you might have got the quotation from the internet and have not checked the full context of the quotation, or are quoting someone who is not a scholar and the quote is therefore not relevant to the topic

A well-used quotation is only a few words long and illustrates a scholar's view. It is likely to be a phrase or term that has been coined but could be a succinct summary of a view.

Presentation

There is nothing worse for an exam marker than turning to an essay to find a thick block of text or illegible handwriting. Most scripts are scanned and marked on-screen, so you need to reflect on what your writing will look like after that process. Some of the worst things I see on-screen are:

→ handwriting that fills the lines so that each line touches the next

→ pens that are too inky and leak through the page, making the text look all blotched

→ tiny handwriting

→ people who write sideways in the margin

If your teacher often comments on your presentation, perhaps now is the time to think again. An essay that cannot be read properly cannot be said to be communicating excellently with the reader. Think about changes you can make, such as:

→ changing pens (remember that you have to write in black in an exam)

→ slowing down your writing speed while you practise essays (you will speed up as you train yourself to be neater)

→ writing more often in class — don't give your writing hand a shock in the exam season

→ leaving a line between paragraphs

Conversely, if you are breaking down your major PACE paragraphs into shorter minor paragraphs, it is important not to end up with what looks like a bullet-point list. You need to come across as an academic writer, not a list-maker.

The examiner

Believe it or not, your examiner is not trying to catch you out. Essay questions are set so that you can demonstrate what you know about some aspect of the specification. Essays can be broad or narrow — that is, on a topic or on a specific aspect of a topic. With the right preparation, you will not be surprised by anything you get in the exam. The wording of subject-specific phrases must come from your specification, too.

The questions on the exam paper are composed by a team of examiners who have the relevant experience to write them. This

> **! Common pitfall**
> The style that examiners are looking for is academic. It is important not to try to joke with the examiner or come across as too pretentious. Imagine you are having a conversation with an older stranger when deciding where to pitch your tone.

> **! Common pitfall**
> You might be surprised that the exams don't always test equal amounts of Year 1 and Year 2 material. This is a big misunderstanding — there is no requirement for any of the material to be taught in a particular year, so all the questions could come from any part of the specification. Therefore, there is no such thing as Year 1 or Year 2 material.

team also prepares a mark scheme for each question at the same time. Sample mark schemes or those for past papers are published online. It is important to remember that mark schemes in a subject like religious studies can never give a definitive list of what is expected in an answer. However, they are very useful to you, the student, because they can give you an idea about what might come up and the level of detail expected.

When the exam has been sat, a group of senior examiners decides how the exam will be marked that year and then trains the full team of examiners to mark accordingly. This basically means that they decide how the levels of response are going to be applied to this year's questions — what is going to be a 'good' essay and what will be an 'excellent' one, and so on.

So, your examiner is going to be one of these people, all trained in the same way. They will often be a teacher who is experienced in working with A-level students and genuinely wants learners at that level to do well and will truly get excited over a great script in front of them. Remember that they are all human beings and, like your teacher, will prefer good presentation over poor presentation.

The examiner will be marking a great many scripts in a row so do not give them a reason to dread marking yours. Always assume that yours will be marked late at night and so be as clear as you possibly can. Crucially, the examiner knows that you had only a limited amount of time and will be used to reading essays of this length. They know what to look for in that context, so do not worry.

Levels of response

As you know, the levels of response are tiers of comments or descriptors that an examiner uses to determine your grade. They have to match the essay they have just read to the appropriate level descriptors. Due to their training, they will quickly have a good idea about which level (or band) to put your answer into, but you need to leave them in no doubt that it will be the top level! Levels are also determined differently for AO1 and AO2, so if the question tests both skills, you need to make sure your answer meets the top level for each.

The common features of the highest levels — and therefore what you need to demonstrate in your writing — are shown in Table 3.4.

Table 3.4 Example levels of response for the top grades in A-level religious studies

AO1	AO2
• Focused on the question — deploys the right information to answer the specific question, not just things relevant to the topic. • Accurate and detailed — not from length or quantity but through deployment of 'just enough'. • Precise — technical terms are used when they can be (and not just for the sake of it). • References to scholars or their views are used where necessary and appropriate. • A range of views is given — not just a narrow focus — but remaining specific to the question.	• Clear, successful, authoritative argument that runs through an essay and that covers the key points — it is thorough. • Confident analysis that really engages with the material and shows perception. • Skilful structure that comes from excellent planning and a clear line of argument — sustained throughout the whole essay. • Use of scholars or scholarly views within the critical analysis. • The essay is holistic — arguments lead to reasoned judgements at the end.

Positive marking

Examiners are trained to mark positively, so they will be constantly trying to justify giving you more marks or a higher level. This means that the odd mistake won't bring you down, but the essay is considered holistically.

When they have decided on the level, the examiner needs to decide how far into that level the essay goes. They might use the bullet points in the level descriptors almost as a checklist, so if your essay can be said to fulfil them all, they won't have any choice but to give you all the marks.

Activity

Go through a paragraph in your last essay and see if you can justify ticking off every point in Table 3.4. Would you have persuaded an examiner to give you all the marks? Of course, you can try to improve it if you need to.

Scholarly views

Much is made of the many scholars you need to study in A-level religious studies. The danger in studying too many is that your work becomes AO1-focused and you are constantly learning what different people said, rather than engaging with them critically.

All exam boards expect you to be able to explore a range of views about each topic. Being able to namedrop and supply appropriate quotations for each one, however, is not necessarily the way to the highest marks. Being in confident control of the material is enough.

Scholarly views or academic approaches, therefore, or the ideas of scholarship, refer to the views a scholar might hold, whether or not you know their name. Just make sure you know the views of the scholars named on the specification.

! Common pitfall

Some essays seem to have a target number of scholars to mention. The best essays, however, answer the question, offering scholarly views only to maintain a line of argument.

The written essay — what next?

Your essay is not finished when it's written. First, when you can, you should take a break and re-read the essay before submitting it. You should also reflect on how you found the process of writing it:

→ Was it easy to come up with a line of argument?
→ Was the research element of the preparation straightforward? Are your notes clear and up-to-date?
→ Could you answer the essay again? In an exam situation?

As you reflect, if you are honest with yourself, you will be able to work out what should come next. Perhaps you need to ask your teacher about aspects of your notes — or go back to the textbook one last time. Perhaps you need to note the topic down as one to revise in more detail when it comes to it — and so on.

There are plenty of ways that you can improve your essay skills after you receive it back, marked and with comments. Don't forget that you are on a 2-year journey and each piece of work you get back should contribute to your next one being better, even if it is on a different topic. Don't forget, too, that being on a 2-year journey gives you time to correct — and then master — one skill at a time, so make sure you don't end up trying to run before you can walk.

Teacher feedback

When you get an essay back, you will receive it with a mark and some comments. Remember, your teacher is your greatest source of help and your most important tool to success, so both the mark and the comments are helpful. However, it is also useful to have your own exam board's levels of response available to you to help you to reflect.

The mark

The mark will hopefully indicate any breakdown between the AO1 and AO2 points. Reflect on two things and note down your reflections somewhere — perhaps at the top of the essay:

→ Is the mark typical for you? If it is lower than usual, what went wrong? If it is higher, what did you do differently?

→ How could you have got one mark more for each AO point? If you were not at the top of the level, which aspects of the level did you not fulfil and what aspect of the level above could you try to work on to improve?

The comments

Your teacher will have identified any inaccuracies and made general comments for improvement. Proper use of that feedback can make a huge amount of difference to your progress over time. Make sure you engage fully with each comment — perhaps ticking it off on your essay when you have — and going back to ask for clarification if needed.

Corrections

One good habit to get into is to use your reflections on the essay and the feedback you have been given to try to make corrections to the essay you have been given back.

→ Knowledge inaccuracies can be looked up and amended — but if the mistake came from your notes then don't forget to change your notes, too.

→ Issues with your explanations can be rewritten; again, if your notes weren't clear, change them at the same time.

→ If you struggled to give useful arguments for and against, you could re-plan the essay.

→ If you did well, you can think about how you could take it one step further; for example, further research on a scholar.

You can also use this stage to make a to-do list for later in the term, perhaps identifying topics you want to read about further.

> **! Common pitfall**
>
> If you adopt the corrections technique, don't fall into the trap of overworking. It is important to focus on improving one thing at a time, not to rewrite every essay in full.

Classmates

Other members of the class will usually have done the same essay as you and as such they are an invaluable source of information. Perhaps they got something right that you didn't quite understand. Perhaps you could swap essays to help to explore the feedback together.

Other activities you could consider include:

→ Read someone else's completed essay, then try to make a plan for the essay and identify their line of argument.

→ Break down or highlight a paragraph of their essay to explore their paragraph structure. Did they use a PACE structure?

→ Rewrite one of their paragraphs using your own structure but making sure that you only use the same set of information and arguments.

→ Try to re-plan their essay using your line of argument rather than theirs.

→ Get someone to read through some of the more complicated sentences in your essay and to repeat the argument back verbally — was it clear enough?

If you do get some help from a friend, don't forget to offer your help in return as well as take advice.

Future essays

Take time to reflect on the next essay. Remember you are trying with each new essay to make one key improvement. Every mark in A-level religious studies needs to be fought for. When you have decided what you will improve in the next essay, make sure you note it down and review that note before you begin writing the next essay (so that it is fresh in your mind).

Another thing to reflect on for the future is timing. If your essay was a homework essay, think about whether you could have managed the same title in the relevant amount of time for your exam. If not, why not? What would your major paragraphs have been if you'd been restricted in time?

If it was a timed essay, did you leave enough time for an effective conclusion? If you have just done a mock exam, were you disciplined about timing?

> **! Common pitfall**
>
> Don't let yourself down by not timing yourself properly — if your last essay on an exam paper is too short, you will lose a disproportionate number of marks.

Greatness

You will have seen that the best essays incorporate authority, clear command of the material and precision. When you achieve these, you will bring with you a personal style that is your voice — and this is a precious thing to have. This section tries to bring together some of the key tips from the whole 2-year journey to help you write the best essays.

The plan

The plan is the make-or-break moment in essay writing and it ensures that you:

→ follow your line of argument throughout the whole essay

→ present a balanced discussion before reaching your judgement

→ keep to time if necessary

→ don't forget any AO1 points that you need to incorporate

These are the most important few minutes that you will spend in an exam. Try to plan all the essays at the start of the exam to help you calm your nerves and to get your brain thinking while you write. Getting any one of the above points wrong could drop you to a B grade or below.

Own your line of argument

Equally, your line of argument must be something that you are prepared to claim for yourself because that will ensure that your voice and your authority are clear in your writing. In order to do that, you need to:

- → be clear about the topic by having explored every aspect of it from the specification (and beyond)
- → read widely about the topic and particular aspects of the topic
- → engage fully in class discussion
- → be prepared to change your mind during your 2-year course (but not during the exam)
- → understand other lines of argument and know why you think you reject them at this stage

Remember that you are aiming to be able to go into an exam, see the questions in front of you and know what your line of argument is without much thought. However, if you BUG the question (see p. 32), you will ensure that you don't rush into it and accidentally come up with a line of argument that has nothing to do with what that specific question is asking.

Practice essays

Practice makes perfect and the completion of practice essays is obviously central to being successful in an exam as this is the way that you are assessed in religious studies. It trains you to get as close to automatic as you possibly can — but don't overdo it and burn yourself out. Some other practice ideas include:

- → Give yourself 8–10 minutes to write a perfect PACE paragraph — either using a specific title or re-doing one from class.
- → Turn a homework essay into a timed essay.
- → Plan answers to an essay title in 2–3 minutes as if in an exam.

Think higher

We have seen that, however ambitious you are, it is important to understand the process (or journey) of moving step by step towards the higher grades, fixing one thing at a time. However, here we are considering higher thinking skills that can help to ensure that your processing of your religious studies information is kept fresh and alive. Once information is understood and applied, three skills remain that in many ways match the descriptions of higher-level answers that we have been talking about. Thinking briefly about the theory will help you at all stages of your course and will ensure that you push everything you do to the highest levels — class discussion, reading and writing. The three skills are:

- → **Analysis** — can you sort information, compare topics or ideas, make links, question concepts and take them deeper, dissecting them and seeking inferences?
- → **Evaluation** — can you argue for and against, defend both your views and those of others, balance approaches and reach judgements, exploring the importance of the opinions you cover?
- → **Creation** — can you formulate your own ideas, work out how to investigate things further yourself, design your own argument and imagine a new application of a theory to an area different from that in class?

> **! Common pitfall**
>
> In a quest to be original, you might mistakenly think that choosing an extreme point of view and arguing for it, come what may, will draw attention to your answers. It is better to be realistic about what you really believe, even if you agree with the majority.

Take it further

The three high-order thinking skills of analysis, evaluation and creation are the highest parts of Bloom's learning taxonomy. Use a search engine to explore this further. Try to decide how successful you are at the different stages of learning.

Two example essays

Below are two example essays. The first is, a good example of an essay that could be written in about 40 minutes. The second is a developing essay that has plenty of areas for improvement. It is slightly shorter but the framework is right for a 40-minute essay. You might like to cover up the annotations first to see what your comments would have been.

Annotated example 3.13

To what extent is the Ontological Argument successful in proving the existence of God?

A line of argument is established in the plan. Given the student's approach, the Ontological Argument (as an a priori argument) will be said to be unsuccessful.

Plan

LOA: a priori arguments do not work in proving God's existence.

Successful	Not successful
God is a special case and so the argument works — Anselm start.	Defines things into existence — Gaunilo/ Kant 1st objection.
Works without using our experience which can deceive us — Anselm detail.	Existence is not a proper predicate — Kant 2nd objection.

Due to careful planning, the student knows that the a priori approach will be central to their essay and so ensures it is present in the introduction.

Essay

The Ontological Argument, put forward by Anselm as a prayer and Descartes independently several hundred years later, uses an a priori approach to try to prove God's existence, thus differing from many other arguments. We shall see that Anselm's argument, while not defeated by Gaunilo, is weak simply as an a priori argument and that, as demonstrated by Kant, such arguments can never prove God's existence.

The argument's key strength could be said to be its reliance on the fact that God is a special case

The student shows context, a timeline and the key scholars in favour of the Ontological Argument.

Shows the bigger picture: the Ontological Argument versus other arguments.

Introduces the scholars against the argument.

Analyse. A relevant amount of information is introduced to keep the paragraph flowing.

The language of the essay is forceful but not judgemental.

The student recognises the need to explain Anselm's argument concisely for this essay and has planned to do this in this paragraph, which is why the first paragraph was shorter.

and so a different type of logic is required. Anselm said that God is 'that than which nothing greater can be conceived' and the idea that God is the greatest possible being might indicate that its logic needs to be different to other attempts to prove God's existence. When dealing with the metaphysical, it is likely that logic used in everyday situations is going to be different. It should be noted, however, that Anselm's *Proslogion* was written as a prayer to God and not as a direct attempt to prove his existence and therefore God's unique nature ends up being used as an excuse to suggest an argument works where, in fact, it does not.

A clear advantage of a priori arguments is the fact that they do not rely on our experience, which we know to differ from person to person and so can be argued to be unreliable. Anselm's first formulation of his argument states that, just like the Fool in the Psalms, all people have a common understanding of God that some reject and some accept. Anselm goes on to observe that a painter's imagination of a painting is different to the painting's existence in reality — there are two types of existence: existence in the mind alone and existence in reality. Anselm states that God exists in everyone's mind — atheist or theist. It is greater to exist in reality than in the mind alone; God, who is the greatest possible being, cannot simply exist in the mind as this would contradict his definition and so God must exist in both the mind and reality — and so God must exist. In his second formulation, Anselm says that there are two types of being — necessary and contingent beings. Necessary beings that cannot not exist are clearly greater than contingent beings (which we can imagine not existing) and so God, who is the greatest possible being, must be necessary, which means God must exist. Thus, Anselm's argument does

Point. Following the PACE structure, a point is made to guide the paragraph.

Criticise. A positive point is given to back up Anselm's view.

Criticise. A negative point is given to continue the discussion about the original point and to keep the paragraph flowing.

Evaluate. The paragraph is brought back to the point and also to the essay title.

not use observations or experience of the world to argue. The argument seems internally coherent but it ignores the fact that we can have unreal things in our minds that, even if we believe them, do not become real — such as Gaunilo's example of gossip. Equally, Gaunilo observed that there is a real difference between the imagined painting and the final product. We know that different people have different pictures in their mind when the same words are spoken. It seems, therefore, that however internally consistent Anselm's argument is, the fact that it does not rely on experience does not lead to the conclusion that it is successful.

Indeed, a key weakness of the argument is that it seems to define things into existence. Gaunilo used the argument of a perfect island to illustrate this in 'On Behalf of the Fool'. He said that we might imagine the greatest conceivable lost island somewhere in the ocean and if we were told about it, we might well be able to imagine it. However, simply because it is in the mind does not mean that it is in reality as well because nobody had demonstrated its existence in the first place. The idea behind Gaunilo's point is important because it shows the need to look externally to consider the notion of existence, but Anselm successfully rejected Gaunilo's logic in 'In Reply to Gaunilo' by redirecting him to the fact that God is a special case, not like an island, which is contingent. Kant seems to make the point more successfully, however, by using the example of a triangle. A triangle might be said to be a triangle because it has internal angles that add up to 180 degrees but the triangle only has these angles if it exists in the first place. There is therefore no proof in a priori arguments of God's existence because they only work if God exists in the first place.

Relevant scholarship is used — it is possible to get high marks in A-level religious studies simply from excellent use of the thinkers listed on the specification.

The overall essay remains in line with the line of argument stated in the introduction.

Kant is used as a development of the paragraph in the criticise part of the paragraph.

Can you identify the PACE structure of this paragraph?

The argument may further be rejected on the basis that it misunderstands the nature of existence as a predicate. Kant believed that existence is not a determining predicate, that is, it does not add anything to our understanding of a subject. Kant uses the example of 100 thalers (a type of currency) to say that 100 real thalers is exactly the same amount of money as 100 possible thalers — we know how many coins that would be. However, to say 100 thalers exists tells us nothing new about the thalers. Equally, we could use the example of a unicorn. We could say that a unicorn has a horn and is white and is magical and we know something more about the unicorn; however, we could not say that the unicorn exists because that tells us nothing new about it. Kant's approach does seem to reject the entire logic of the Ontological Argument and, although it could be rejected on the grounds that contingent and necessary existence are different because to say something exists necessarily *does* add information about that thing, it seems that any attempt to talk about different types of existence is simply playing with words and so the criticism of the argument seems to stand.

Although the essay is going to reject the Ontological Argument, it shows an openness to the other side.

Ultimately, the Ontological Argument's resurgence in recent years has opened the possibility to it successfully proving the existence of God. However, in no version does it successfully overcome the core challenge of how it attempts to use words to create an object — to define something into existence — and therefore it seems necessary to reject it as an argument for God's existence, perhaps in favour of a posteriori arguments.

This conclusion goes a bit wider to suggest what would essentially be the next step in research.

Annotated example 3.14

Evaluate the view that utilitarianism continues to offer a useful way of resolving moral dilemmas.

Plan

LOA: utilitarianism is a nice idea but not realistic in reality.

Does continue to offer a useful way	Does not continue to offer a useful way
Allows us to balance complex situations because it is objective — hedonic calculus.	With scientific advances, utilitarianism is no longer as helpful — Act Utilitarianism.
Does not need to be taken at face value — Mill.	Does not value human life intrinsically.

The plan does not seem to offer direct points in favour of, or against, the title in each of the four boxes. The points are valid but it will be hard for the student to keep focused on the question.

Essay

Utilitarianism is a major ethical theory that has a number of different forms. The key forms in this essay will be the views of Bentham and Mill. I will argue that utilitarianism is not a realistic ethical theory in any form, although it makes some sense.

A valid start but it does not fully engage with the specifics of the essay title.

This introduction is using the CBA technique (see p.38). How could you improve it?

Some people might say that utilitarianism is not as helpful as it was before because with modern scientific advances going so rapidly, it is not clear what the future holds. Act Utilitarianism is the idea that we should make each decision based on the moment and that involves predicting the future. One key weakness of utilitarianism is that it is very difficult to use because we cannot know the future. This means we cannot accurately decide what will benefit the majority. For example, we cannot know what use it will be to have stored embryos in the future because we do not know what they will be able to be used for in the future. We can develop this point by saying that we do not know how we should measure pleasure or pain. A weakness of this point is that

It is especially useful in ethics to give an illustration or case study without spending too much time on it.

This sentence needs developing. It is the criticise part of the PACE structure. The student is trying to point out that pleasure and pain are arguably difficult to measure because we do not know, especially when thinking into the future, what will turn out to maximise happiness and minimise suffering.

utilitarianism relies on our ability to make decisions each time, which is why it is relativist and so actually the fact that modern scientific advances are happening rapidly means that utilitarianism is best placed to help.

It might seem that the objectivity provided by utilitarianism is a less emotionally involved way of making moral decisions. Bentham's hedonic calculus treats all human life as having equal value and therefore ensures that there is complete separation from personal ties, and decisions can be made purely according to the measure of pleasure and pain. The hedonic calculus is a way of measuring pleasure and pain using seven factors that should be considered when making a moral decision. These factors are things such as the intensity of the pleasure or pain, the duration of it, how soon it will happen (propinquity) and how many people will be affected. This is how Bentham measures the 'greatest happiness for the greatest number'. The hedonic calculus is certainly thorough and ensures that we are thorough when making moral decisions — and it contributes to the theory being seen as straightforward — but it fails as an approach because it is entirely unrealistic in how it is applied. It also could lead to some things being seen as good simply because of a plain majority and might justify sadism. Therefore, utilitarianism's approach might be less emotional but this does not make it useful in resolving moral dilemmas.

Utilitarianism perhaps can be rejected on the grounds of its disinterest in human life and therefore be said not to be a useful ethical theory for modern times. With technology being prioritised in the twenty-first century, it could be argued that humans need to prioritise and protect human life, and an alternative approach that does that might be better, such as natural law, where preservation of life is one of the primary

The weakness is the criticise part, which leads into evaluation. However, the evaluation seems to contradict the student's line of argument and they perhaps should have developed it briefly to be clearer that even if Act Utilitarianism allows for rapid changes in society, it is still very unrealistic to go through the process each time.

This paragraph is much better written than the previous major paragraph. The point of the paragraph is clear and the PACE structure well-established. It often happens that essays warm up as they progress. It is important for you to consider how you will hit the ground running and be consistently good throughout.

The final major paragraph is a strength. Given the student wishes to argue against the theory, perhaps the order of paragraphs needed rethinking. This shows how 'make or break' the one or two minutes spent planning the essay can be.

While always valid, this is the third time that the student has used the idea of the rapid change of the twenty-first century. It makes the essay rather repetitive and could have been avoided with better planning.

The evaluation part of the paragraph is slightly stilted because you will have noticed that the point of the paragraph is not clearly stated. This is a common error. The best points will be clear arguments for or against which guide the paragraph.

precepts. For example, utilitarianism will allow abortion and euthanasia very easily and it will quickly make the decision to kill some lives if others might be saved — seen, for example, in the trolley problem. This is a strong point because many would argue that, whether or not you are religious, there is something intrinsically different and special about human life and its ability to reason and its place on the planet. I think this is a further demonstration of the unreliability of the theory and a form of utilitarianism that might work would be one that shows more regard for people.

A final strength of utilitarianism is shown by Mill's approach. Mill believed that Act Utilitarianism was too naïve in its approach and needed to be applied in the context of society and collective decisions, rather than individuals and each unique decision. Thus, Mill believed we should create rules that use utilitarian principles for society. These are rules that are generally kept and sometimes broken if needed, so Mill's approach is one of 'rules of thumb' rather than strict rules. However, rules might be said to clash, especially as society advances, and, as we have seen, society is changing rapidly. Therefore, Mill's approach does not seem to offer a modern way of making moral decisions.

Overall, utilitarianism is strong in theory but unrealistic in practice. I therefore conclude that it is not a useful way of resolving moral dilemmas, such as in business ethics when difficult decisions may need to be made that keep a business focused on its core mission statement even though the majority of customers might want it to change.

There are some interesting points in this paragraph. If Bentham and Mill are the only scholars on this student's specification then it would be understandable why they might not be able to show awareness of other types of utilitarianism. However, the A-grade student might well have read around the subject sufficiently so that they are not quite as dismissive as this student.

Perhaps realising how repetitive they have been, the student here introduces new material in the conclusion, which serves only to dilute the conclusion and therefore the essay as a whole. The student has clearly got many good points to make and the essay would have looked very different had it been properly planned from the outset.

You should know

> How to approach different types of essay encountered throughout your 2-year course.

> How to deconstruct a question quickly and effectively through the BUG technique and understanding the command words and phrases.

> The central importance of an essay plan and establishing a clear line of argument.

> The CBA, PEEL, PACE and conclusion writing techniques.

> How to improve the style of your writing and how best to impress the examiner.

> How to use reflection and feedback after you have finished writing the essay to help you turn your B-grade essays into A* ones.

4 How to revise

Learning objectives

> To reflect on your strengths and weaknesses when revising
> To be clear on what you are aiming for in the exam
> To consider a range of revision techniques
> To know how you are going to revise

If you remember the dread of GCSE revision, then don't forget the relief of having finished the exams. The good news is that at A-level, you are hopefully studying fewer subjects, and ones that you have chosen, so revision should be less of a chore. To make it even less exhausting, if you have followed the study advice in the book throughout the course, you should have less to do than you would otherwise.

Know yourself

Of course, revision doesn't just start at the end of your course. You will have had school exams, unit tests or class essays and so on. As you go through these events, you need to think about what has gone well and what challenges you have faced. Perhaps you revised for one test using mind maps and everything went wrong — so maybe mind maps aren't for you!

Are you a procrastinator? Or are you reluctant to stop working and take a break? Successful revision is about being honest with yourself and knowing when to be more or less strict with your routine. Schedule in rewards when you have earned them. Honesty is also important when testing yourself on material. Does your internal monologue say, 'Yes, I know that!' or, 'I didn't get that right; I need to do it again'? Find ways of motivating yourself, such as putting up a picture of the university you want to go to in front of your workspace. Amid all this, eat healthily, exercise, get fresh air, sleep well and clear your mind with mindfulness techniques or whatever works for you.

What type of learner are you? This might help you to work out what type of revision you might be best at. Broadly, there are three types of learner:

→ Visual — word-focused activities, mind maps, colour coding
→ Auditory — perhaps flashcards which you can read out loud
→ Kinaesthetic — smaller bursts of activities, planning paragraphs, sorting flashcards into groups

> **! Common pitfall**
>
> Don't assume that the techniques you used at GCSE will transfer automatically to A-level. The demands of the A-level course are different: more information, more analysis and so on are required.

Activity

Use an internet search engine to find a quiz on your learning style and be aware of this as you pick which advice to follow in this chapter.

Know the exam

In order to carry out any activity, you need to know what you are aiming towards. If you have made topic notes throughout the course, then obviously you know you need to learn these, but how are you going to store the information in your brain so that it is appropriately accessible? One way is by knowing the exam and the type of question you will face when accessing the information. (The final section in this book gives details about each exam board's requirements, although you will hopefully know these well in advance.)

For example, if your board has split essays (comprising AO1 and AO2 questions), you will need to be able to explain a theory or scholar's view in the appropriate amount of time. However, if you are preparing for unified essays, then the knowledge and understanding have to be interlaced with your arguments and you should learn these together.

If your teacher hasn't already given it to you, download the specification from your exam board's website and print off the pages relevant to you. Every word that is not in a 'suggested' section or 'for example' sentence can appear on an exam paper. Make sure you really can answer questions on the whole specification.

As you revise, make sure that you can answer any kind of question on a topic. For example, if you have revised natural law thoroughly, you should be able to answer:

→ an evaluation question on whether natural law is relevant today
→ a question asking you if the weaknesses of natural law outweigh the strengths
→ a question asking you to apply natural law to an aspect of practical ethics
→ a question asking you to compare natural law with another theory

You will have done enough essays throughout your course to be able to sit down and work out any possible question. Remember that when setting questions, examiners are never trying to catch you out, so the questions will be as accessible as possible. Any 'difficult' terms will only be those on the specification, which you should have learned.

Planning your revision time

Make a timetable or a schedule for your revision — and stick to it! Start sensibly early — perhaps in time for your mock exams. You will have revised for these, so use the feedback from them to get yourself into a habit of working nice and early. It is useful to break your subjects down into smaller chunks, rather than revising a whole topic at a time. That way you will have a sense of relief when you finish a chunk and won't resent moving on to another.

! Common pitfall

With boards where you get a choice of question, don't let yourself down by 'dropping' a topic. If that topic comes up, you will be left with no choice on the paper and if another question you are forced to do is phrased unexpectedly then you will be stuck. The specification may initially seem daunting, but it will be manageable for an A-level student.

✓ Exam tip

Some questions for the Edexcel and CCEA exam boards require you to make an explicit link to different areas of the specification, whereas AQA combines different areas of the specification as part of the course. Depending on your exam board, make sure you are fully prepared for this and that you draw out the links in your revision notes.

Your main revision will, of course, start during the Easter holidays (but don't forget to rest and relax as well). Make sure that you have all your notes in place at the start of the holiday, ready to be learned. See if you can cover the whole course over that holiday period. Mix up the papers so that you are not doing all of philosophy then all of ethics, for example, and try to revise more than one of your subjects each day.

The first half of the summer term will be an opportunity to ask your teacher questions that have come up during the holiday revision. You should also aim to cover the whole course again independently, which seems daunting but is achievable as you will be reminding yourself more than learning from scratch.

Then, as exam time looms, you should switch to revising in the order of your papers, so make sure you have your timetable to hand.

What to learn

If you have followed the advice in this book then you will already have sifted through your class notes, textbook notes and further reading notes and created your ultimate guide to a topic. In this guide you should have covered both AO1 and AO2 points — both facts and information about topics and arguments for and against different themes, theories or big questions. There is likely to be more AO1 than AO2, but the exam carries more marks for AO2.

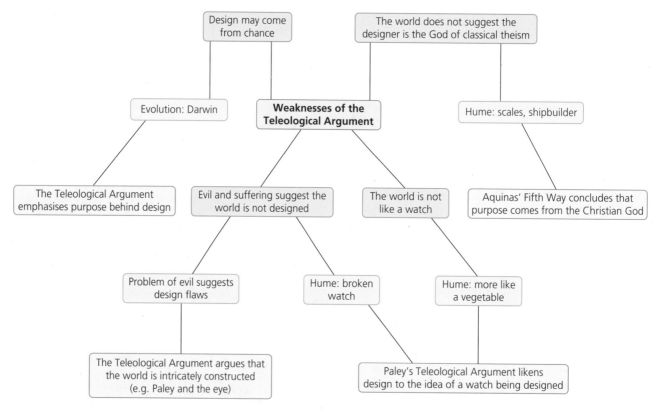

Figure 4.1 Weaknesses of the Teleological Argument — an argument-driven mind map

One way to deal with this imbalance is to revise the arguments for and against first. That way, as you learn the arguments you can begin to shape in your mind how you will introduce relevant AO1 points in an essay situation.

As you make further notes, you should try to focus on the arguments more than the knowledge. So, if you are preparing a mind map on the Teleological Argument, you could put 'weaknesses of the Teleological Argument' at the centre of the mind map. In the example in Figure 4.1, you can see the outer layers contain the basic AO1 material.

It cannot be repeated often enough: make sure you learn the *entire* specification.

Case studies and scripture

For some aspects of the course, you will need to know some case studies, especially in ethics topics. When studying religious beliefs, you will have encountered a range of scriptural passages and examples to explore different points. The key here is not to overdo it. All you will need to do in the exam is to explain or illustrate points using scripture. So, if your class studied several business models for business ethics that all illustrated the same thing, only learn the details of one of them. If you found five Bible passages to illustrate Christian exclusivism, then be selective about which you take into the exam. Are there examples that can be used in more than one topic or sub-topic?

How to learn

There is a lot more to revision than just knowing the techniques — you need to work out which ones are the best for you. You may have already found a technique that helped you through the mock exams — or you may be reading this before your mocks. Of the ideas suggested below, you might have tested and discarded some of them already (try them again if you discarded them in Year 8) and some might be a complete revelation to you.

Now is the time to put away your devices — not just to avoid distractions but also because the best revision takes place with pen and paper. Pen and paper:

→ slows you down and gives you time to process what you are writing
→ avoids the automated nature of typing
→ prepares you for exams when you are going to be writing

Practise working in increasing lengths of time as well: your exams are going to be lengthy affairs.

Create materials

It is a myth that reading through your notes or the textbook counts as revision. Reading is passive — as is mindless copying out. Creating materials is a higher skill that will train your brain to remember information and arguments. Creating different types of material will give your brain the opportunity to remember information in different ways and will allow you to access it from a number of different angles when you are in the exam. You could create mind maps, essay plans, diagrams, flow charts... the possibilities are as many as your imagination can provide.

Test yourself

You need to test yourself regularly throughout your revision. Incorporate ways of testing yourself into each section of work. For example, start each session with a quiz on the previous session — perhaps by summarising five key points from the day before and being reflective about how easy you found them. You can then, if necessary, make a note to return to the topic soon. When you plan how you are going to test yourself, remember that leaving gaps in time between learning and testing is important because you have to work harder to retrieve the information, which in turn, helps your long-term memory.

Be essay-focused

Not only do you need to know that you can answer any question given to you in an exam but also you need to show yourself that you can do it. Your revision needs to include opportunities for you to practise essays in the right amount of time (and perhaps to get feedback from your teacher). In addition, take time to make copious essay plans so that you can practise manipulating material. That might be a useful way to test yourself at the end of a section of revision.

You don't have to write out full essays all the time. You could practise writing a focused paragraph for or against a title to ensure you are always focused on the end result in the exam, which is a well-crafted essay. Alternatively, you could write your introduction and conclusion and then bullet point each paragraph (or use the PACE structure instead of bullet points), limiting yourself to one side of A4.

Suggested revision techniques
Halving the size

Whether you work by bullet points or mind maps, this technique forces you to recall, be critical and repeat. The actual learning will always be focused on what you do not know, rather than what you remember.

→ Identify your topic. Write down as much as you can remember on an A4 sheet (or A3 mind map).

→ Use a different coloured pen and, referring to your notes or revision book, add to your sheet or mind map and correct it.

→ The next time you return to the topic, allow yourself only half as much space to complete the same activity. As you work, write down the basics and think through (or say aloud) the other things that you would write in an essay when covering that point.

→ The third time you do this, use half as much space again. What you end up with is a very short summary of the topic that can be your key points to look through the night before the exam.

Memory training

Buy a set of flashcards (or cut down card to size). On the front of each flashcard, summarise a sub-topic (or appropriate amount of information) and on the back, write some short-answer test questions on that material. Then set up four or five boxes and label them as shown in Figure 4.2.

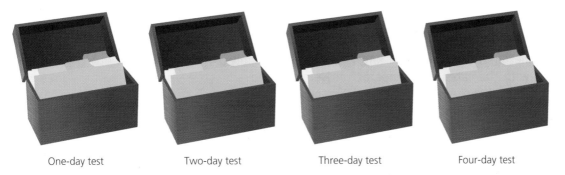

One-day test   Two-day test   Three-day test   Four-day test

Figure 4.2 Flashcard boxes for memory training

When you have done this, place your first flashcard (Figure 4.3) in the 'One-day test' box. This means you return to the flashcard in one day. The next day, test yourself and then recap all the information on the flashcard. Write the date you last tested yourself on the question side. If you pass (and be honest with yourself), put the flashcard in the second box and only return to it after 2 days. After that, if you pass the test then you can move the card up a box and if you fail it then you move it down a box.

The Sheep and the Goats	The Sheep and the Goats
• Jesus comes back at the end of time in judgement	• Who judges? When? Who is judged?
• All people are gathered (judgement of all at the end of time?)	• Who are the sheep and who are the goats?
• He separates the sheep from the goats (not all will be saved)	• On what is judgement based?
• The judgement is based on how they treated others (hungry, thirsty, strangers — salvation on actions; heaven must be earned) (what about faith?)	• How many are saved?
• Eternal life/eternal punishment (heaven and hell as real places)	• What does this teach about heaven and hell?
	• What is the key quotation?
'Truly I tell you, whatever you did for one of the least of these brothers and sisters of mine, you did for me.'	*2 April* *3 April* *5 April*

Front   **Back**

Figure 4.3 Example flashcard

This technique helps you to ensure that topics have been embedded in your long-term memory, not just your short-term memory.

If you prefer to keep your flashcards shorter, you can simply put a command on one side (e.g. 'Five key points about the Sheep and the Goats') and the answer on the other.

Take it further

Find out about other methods of memory enhancement, whether it is an app or game on your phone or something like the method of loci. There are also apps that help you to create flashcards. Do this well in advance of revision time, though, otherwise it just becomes a method of procrastination.

Talking and teaching

If you can teach something, then you must know it. Bore your family at the dinner table with the categorical imperative. Help a friend who is struggling with the concept of secularisation (but don't spend all your time giving to others). Tell your favourite stuffed animal the finer points of reality.

It is also useful to get someone to test you. Being in a test situation increases the pressure slightly and holds you accountable. It also breaks up the boredom of doing everything alone during revision. You can mix this up a bit:

→ If someone knows the subject, then you can test each other as a pair.

→ Try giving yourself 1 minute to talk about a topic while the other person listens and then tries to fill in the gaps afterwards.

→ You could each prepare a different essay plan and mark each other's.

→ If someone does not know the subject, you can give them your revision notes to help.

The ethical rainbow

This technique also works well with mind maps. The point is to force yourself to apply an ethical theory to an area of practical ethics. You begin with the basics of an ethical theory, along with its strengths and weaknesses, and then force yourself to apply each thing you have written to an aspect of practical ethics. You can make a master rainbow template for each theory and copy it enough times for all the different aspects of practical ethics. A master template for situation ethics might look like Figure 4.4.

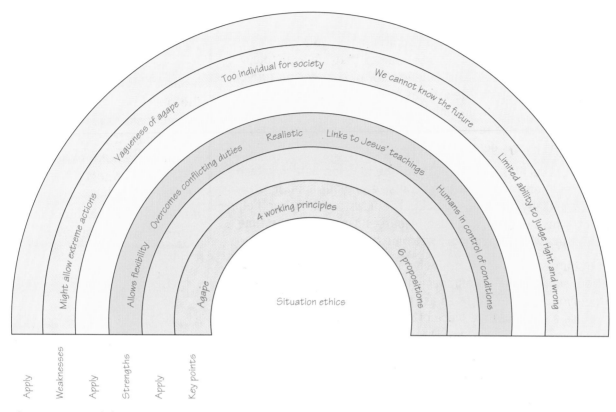

Figure 4.4 A rainbow master template for situation ethics

When applied to euthanasia, the rainbow might look like Figure 4.5.

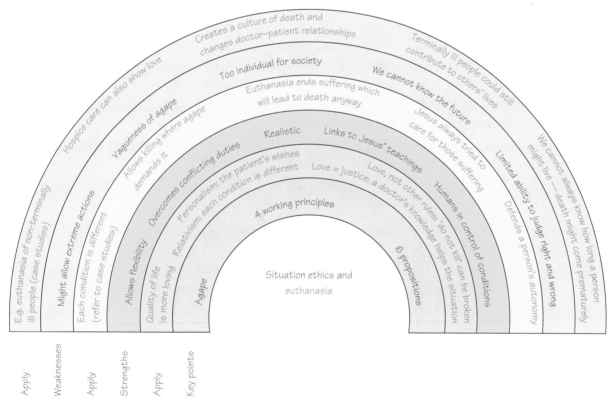

Figure 4.5 A rainbow for situation ethics as applied to euthanasia

Other resources

Having said that you should stick to pen and paper, you can break your revision up a bit by using other resources that are available. Published revision guides will have done a lot of condensing for you, although they should always be used as a checklist rather than your starting point as otherwise you might not have enough material to write a full essay. Online revision guides are similar, although their material has not always been written by experts.

Using resources such as podcasts or YouTube revision guides (which are sometimes prepared by teachers) can stretch your mind in other ways and, especially for ethics, reading the news regularly can help. Getting into the habit of using such resources can extend the time you are revising while providing a welcome break from your desk.

A great resource is your class. Your classmates can provide motivation, support and encouragement. You could set up a group chat where you take it in turns to ask tricky questions about the course or use a collaborative piece of software to make revision notes together — just make sure that you personalise those notes by hand in the long run.

> ### ! Common pitfall
>
> You may think of revision as a one-off activity. However, the best revision comes from constant review across the 2 years. If early Year 1 topics are not looked at again until almost the end of Year 2, it will become a matter of re-teaching yourself, not revision.

You should know

> - That revision is different for everyone, so you need to match your needs with the techniques suggested.
> - That the most effective revision is about being active and creating materials, and using a mix of activities.
> - How to revise in layers — the more you do, the more it builds up in your memory so that you can access the information successfully in the exam.
> - The importance of knowing what you are revising for — knowing what the exam will look like and how you will be best prepared for it.
> - The importance of learning the entire specification.
> - That the best revision techniques will be decided well in advance of the final revision season — experiment with them throughout the course.

5 Exam skills

Before the exam

Having prepared carefully during the revision period, it is important to make sure that when you get to the exam you are in the right frame of mind, otherwise it will all go to waste. Although you are likely to look over some last-minute revision notes, these should not be detailed notes, just refreshers.

→ Make sure you sleep well the night before the exam.

→ Eat properly on the day of the exam, although be aware that high-carbohydrate meals can make some people drowsy.

→ Do not spend time looking on social media to see how much others around the country are dreading the exam.

→ Make sure your pencil case is ready — it should be clear and without any words or logos on it. Don't forget your black pens and highlighters if you use them, although it is better to do everything in pen so that the examiner is convinced that you are utterly in control of the question from the outset.

 Exam tip

Make sure your pens are not brand new and so work smoothly. They should be of a style you are used to writing with so that you can write neatly and quickly. Take spares so that you don't run out of ink half way through a paper.

During the exam

Make sure that you listen carefully to the instructions given by the invigilator, even if it is the last exam in a long series. Treat each exam as if it is the first and you will find that you are fresher in your approach to the later ones.

Turning the page

The moment you turn the page over, you might be excited, or you might feel you have forgotten everything you know. Both reactions are normal, and both reactions are found in top-grade students.

→ If you are the excitable type, slow down. Be clear which questions you are going to answer — circle them on the question paper, if it helps.

→ If you panic, look up and down again, breathe in and try using your pen or finger to point to the words of the questions to help you focus.

The main decision you may have to make is which questions to choose (if your board gives you a choice). Do not assume that because your favourite topic has come up, it is the question for you. It might have a slant that you hadn't thought of. If you are struggling to pick a question, then BUG all the questions in the section (see p.32) and as you do so your decision might be made for you. The key thing is not to pick a question based only on the topic, but to pick one based on the whole wording.

Timing is everything

If you mess up your timings, you could quite easily give away two grades' worth of marks. Adding an extra sentence will not get you as many marks as answering a different question properly. You need to be disciplined, and to be disciplined, you need to be well-trained. Timing will have been a key part of your preparation and revision and you should be able to answer different questions automatically. In the exam, make no exception. Write down on the top of your paper the times to start and finish each essay. Stop when your time is up. If all is going well, stopping when your time is up will be easy because you will have just finished the answer.

Be absolutely clear how long you have for each question before you go into the exam, especially for exam boards where different papers have different demands. Don't forget to factor in time to choose your questions (if you have a choice) and to plan them all.

After the exam

Whatever happens in the exam, once you have to stop, you have to stop. It is over and it cannot be changed. Move on — you will either have another exam to think about or celebrations to begin.

You are very likely to unpick questions with your friends or want to rush to find your teacher to tell them what you did and ask if it was right. This isn't helpful, especially in a subject like religious studies where the argument is key and you can choose from endless evidence. Keep off social media, which is always full of memes about how unfair the paper was, and move on.

However, once you have finished your A-level in religious studies, I hope you won't move on entirely and will always remain something of a theologian, philosopher or ethicist.

> **! Common pitfall**
>
> You may find yourself rushing into picking a question because you noticed a topic name you like and just beginning to write. This is throwing all the good techniques of planning out of the window.

You should know

> - **How to prepare yourself properly for the exam.**
> - **How to focus on picking the right questions.**
> - **How important it is to be disciplined when it comes to timing.**
> - **That once the exam is over you have other things to think about.**

Exam board focus

Learning objectives

> To understand the exam structure of your examination board
> To know how to prepare for your examination papers

This section looks at the particular requirements of each of the exam boards and provides some tips specific to your board. We have seen how it is important to be clear about your goals before you embark on anything and so ensuring you know how your final assessment will look is also important. Look at past papers on the exam boards' websites to be absolutely clear.

Remember... the exam is there not just as a horrendous test. It is there so that you can show off the fruit of all your work of the previous 2 years.

Activity

After you have read the section on your exam board, go to its website and look at the resources available there. Here are some points to consider.

- Look at past papers and check that you are clear about the length of the paper as well as the number of marks for each question.
- You could also look at each paper and check you know which questions you would do if you were sitting the paper.
- Look at the example mark schemes and see if you would be able to make the points listed in the mark scheme. Remember that mark schemes are only lists of possible content, so if you were to approach a question differently, that is likely to be fine.
- Some exam boards have example essays or candidate responses from previous years. Look at the commentary provided by the examiners.
- Use the specification to find the papers you are doing. You could print off these pages and use them as a checklist to monitor your learning and/or revision.

AQA

The papers
For AQA, you sit two papers.

Paper 1: Philosophy of religion and ethics
This paper is 3 hours long and is worth 50% of the A-level. There are 100 marks available for the paper. You can see how the questions are divided down in the table overleaf.

Section	Requirements	Marks
A: Philosophy of religion	Two questions each made up of an AO1 essay and an AO2 essay	50
B: Ethics	Two questions each made up of an AO1 essay and an AO2 essay	50

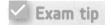

> **✓ Exam tip**
>
> Make sure you plan all your answers and do them in a logical order so that you do not find yourself mis-timing a 3-hour paper.

Paper 2: Religion and dialogues

This paper is 3 hours long and is worth 50% of the A-level. There are 100 marks available for the paper. You can see how the questions are divided in the table below.

Section	Requirements	Marks
A: Christianity	Two questions each made up of an AO1 essay and an AO2 essay	50 (10 + 15 for each question)
B: The dialogue between philosophy and the religion studied	One question from a choice of two — one unified essay	25
C: The dialogue between ethics and the religion studied	One question from a choice of two — one unified essay	25

There are different options for this paper, depending on the religion you have studied:

→ Paper 2A — Buddhism and dialogues
→ Paper 2B — Christianity and dialogues
→ Paper 2C — Hinduism and dialogues
→ Paper 2D — Islam and dialogues
→ Paper 2E — Judaism and dialogues

Points to note

→ If religious studies is the only subject you do with 3-hour exams, make sure you are ready to maintain your concentration for longer.

→ Allocate no more than 40 minutes to answering each whole question — approximately 15 minutes for the part 1 AO1 questions and approximately 20 minutes for the part 2 AO2 questions.

→ The remaining 20 minutes should be spent planning your answers and should also act as a buffer to help you if you slow down over the course of the long exam.

→ Be disciplined with the time you spend on AO1 essays and AO2 essays. Make sure you are not imbalanced in your approach.

→ The unified dialogues essays for Paper 2 require you to make an explicit link between the religion you have studied and either philosophy (section B) or ethics (section C). Make it a habit to do this in the analysis part of the PACE structure (and often you can discuss both the religion and the dialogue in the criticise part).

→ It is only in the dialogues essays (Paper 2, sections B and C) that you get a choice of essay. All other essays are compulsory. However, AQA uses fewer command words.

> **⚠ Common pitfall**
>
> Some students don't practise the two types of essay required for AQA and end up writing unified essays that do not integrate AO1 and AO2. This is where the PACE structure comes in, ensuring you do not simply write out information.

→ Key phrases from the AQA levels of response descriptors for the top grades include:

- Accurate, relevant and fully developed
- Breadth and depth
- Clear and coherent
- Perceptive, precise
- Critical

Edexcel

The papers

For Edexcel, you sit three papers out of a choice of 4. If you sit paper 3, you cannot also sit paper 4B.

Paper 1: Philosophy of religion

This paper is 2 hours long and has 80 marks. It is worth 33.3% of the full A-level. There is no choice on this paper and the paper is structured as shown in the table below.

Section	Requirements	Marks
A: Structured questions	An AO1 question and an AO2 question	8 + 12
B: Anthology question	One question with AO1 and AO2 parts	10 + 20
C: Synoptic question	One unified essay which you must link to one other paper from the course	30

Paper 2: Religion and ethics

This paper is 2 hours long and has 80 marks. It is worth 33.3% of the full A-level. There is no choice on this paper and the paper is structured as shown in the table below.

Section	Requirements	Marks
A: Structured questions	An AO1 question and an AO2 question	8 + 12
B: Anthology question	One question with AO1 and AO2 parts	10 + 20
C: Synoptic question	One unified essay which you must link to one other paper from the course	30

Paper 3: New Testament studies

This paper is 2 hours long and has 80 marks. It is worth 33.3% of the full A-level. There is no choice on this paper and the paper is structured as shown in the table below. If you sit this paper, you cannot also sit the study of Christianity paper (Paper 4B).

Section	Requirements	Marks
A: Structured questions	An AO1 question and an AO2 question	8 + 12
B: Anthology question	One question with AO1 and AO2 parts	10 + 20
C: Synoptic question	One unified essay which you must link to one other paper from the course	30

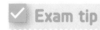 **Exam tip**

With five different types or lengths of essay to master, it is helpful to get into a routine for your Edexcel papers — each paper is the same structure as the others. Make sure you check the number of marks as an additional clarification of the time you need to spend on it.

Paper 4: Study of religion

This paper is 2 hours long and has 80 marks. It is worth 33.3% of the full A-level. There is no choice on this paper and the paper is structured as shown in the table below.

Section	Requirements	Marks
A: Structured questions	An AO1 question and an AO2 question	8 + 12
B: Anthology question	One question with AO1 and AO2 parts	10 + 20
C: Synoptic question	One unified essay which you must link to one other paper from the course	30

You will be entered for one of the following options:
→ Option 4A: Buddhism
→ Option 4B: Christianity
→ Option 4C: Hinduism
→ Option 4D: Islam
→ Option 4E: Judaism
→ Option 4F: Sikhism

If you sit Option 4B, you cannot also sit Paper 3.

Points to note

→ Allow 1 minute per mark but remember that you will also need to allow a few minutes to BUG each question (see p. 32) and plan your essay and prepare your line of argument (for the AO2 and unified essays).
→ Be very disciplined with the time you spend on each question.
→ Remember that in the anthology section, your answer needs to come out of the text. For the AO1 question, this should be reflected in your PEEL structure, and in the AO2 question, this should be reflected in the analyse part of your PACE structure.
→ For the synoptic section, your answer needs to make a direct link to one other paper from the course. This should be reflected in the analyse part of your PACE structure.
→ Remember that all the questions are compulsory.
→ Key phrases from the Edexcel levels of response descriptors for the top grades include:
  ● Range
  ● Critically deconstructs
  ● Connections
  ● Fully justified
  ● Coherent and reasoned
  ● Comprehensive

OCR

The papers

For OCR, Papers 1 and 2 are compulsory and then you have a choice of one paper from Papers 3–7.

Paper 1: Philosophy of religion

This paper is 2 hours long and has 120 marks. It is worth 33.3% of the A-level. There are four questions and you have to answer any three of them. Each question is worth the same as the others and could be on any aspect of the specification.

Paper 2: Religion and ethics

This paper is 2 hours long and has 120 marks. It is worth 33.3% of the A-level. There are four questions and you have to answer any three of them. Each question is worth the same as the others and could be on any aspect of the specification.

Papers 3–7: Developments in religious thought

You do one paper from a choice of different religions offered by OCR:

→ Paper 3 — Christianity
→ Paper 4 — Islam
→ Paper 5 — Judaism
→ Paper 6 — Buddhism
→ Paper 7 — Hinduism

The paper you do is, again, 2 hours long, has 120 marks and is worth 33.3% of the A-level. There are four questions and you have to answer any three of them. Each question is worth the same as the others and could be on any aspect of the specification.

Points to note

→ All OCR essays are unified essays, testing both AO1 and AO2 skills.
→ You should allow about 35 minutes for each essay, with the 15 minutes remaining giving you time to plan all three essays at the start. The fact that they are all the same format is a real advantage in helping you to get into the habit of writing in a particular way.
→ You should have time for four major PACE paragraphs in each essay, each averaging 7 minutes.
→ OCR uses a wide range of command words, so make sure you BUG the question carefully (see p. 32).
→ The papers on the different religions require you to explore issues from within the religion so do not dismiss the beliefs of the religion as being 'untrue' from the outset as you will run out of things to say.
→ Key phrases from the OCR levels of response descriptors for the top grades include:
● Fully comprehends
● Accurate
● Skilfully
● Coherently developed and justified
● Confident

> **! Common pitfall**
> Students sometimes think that two of the OCR questions will come from the first half of the specification and two from the other half. They also sometimes think that if a topic came up one year it will not come up the next. Although examiners never try to catch you out, they also are not allowed to set papers where you could predict the questions in any way.

Eduqas

The papers

The Eduqas exams are offered by the Welsh examination board for students taking exams within English centres. For Eduqas, you sit three papers.

Paper 1: A study of religion

This paper is 2 hours long and has 100 marks. It is worth 33.3% of the A-level. You will be entered for one of the following options:

→ Option A: Christianity
→ Option B: Islam
→ Option C: Judaism
→ Option D: Buddhism
→ Option E: Hinduism
→ Option F: Sikhism

The paper is structured as shown in the table below.

Section	Requirements	Marks
A	One question from a choice of two; part (a) is AO1 and part (b) is AO2	20 + 30
B	One question from a choice of three; part (a) is AO1 and part (b) is AO2	20 + 30

Paper 2: Philosophy of religion

This paper is 2 hours long and has 100 marks. It is worth 33.3% of the A-level. The paper is structured as shown in the table below.

Section	Requirements	Marks
A	One question from a choice of two; part (a) is AO1 and part (b) is AO2	20 + 30
B	One question from a choice of three; part (a) is AO1 and part (b) is AO2	20 + 30

Paper 3: Religion and ethics

This paper is 2 hours long and has 100 marks. It is worth 33.3% of the A-level. The paper is structured as shown in the table below.

Section	Requirements	Marks
A	One question from a choice of two; part (a) is AO1 and part (b) is AO2	20 + 30
B	One question from a choice of three; part (a) is AO1 and part (b) is AO2	20 + 30

! Common pitfall

Students often think that if they have got 5 minutes extra then they should add an extra paragraph. Not only does this look messy but it suggests that an essay hasn't been carefully planned.

Points to note

→ Each of the three papers is structured the same.
→ Allowing 20 minutes for each AO1 question and 30 minutes for AO2 questions will give you time to choose questions and to plan your answers carefully, as well as a slight buffer at the end.

→ Key phrases from the Eduqas levels of response descriptors for the top grades include:
- Extensive and relevant
- Insightful
- Confident
- Thorough
- Perceptive

WJEC

The WJEC exams are offered by the Welsh examination board for students taking exams in Wales. The key skills of AO1 and AO2 are the same as for the other boards, although they are phrased differently and the exam assessment looks slightly different. Here we summarise how the assessment works if you do the AS and A-level in Years 1 and 2 of your course.

Year 1

In Year 1 you sit two papers.

Paper 1: An introduction to the study of religion

You will study one religion from a choice of six:
→ Option A: Christianity
→ Option B: Islam
→ Option C: Judaism
→ Option D: Buddhism
→ Option E: Hinduism
→ Option F: Sikhism

This paper is 1 hour 15 minutes long and has 60 marks. It is worth 15% of the final A-level. The paper is structured as shown in the table below.

Section	Requirements	Marks
A	One question from a choice of two; part (a) is AO1 and part (b) is AO2	15 + 15
B	One question from a choice of three; part (a) is AO1 and part (b) is AO2	15 + 15

Paper 2: An introduction to religion and ethics and the philosophy of religion

This paper is 1 hour 45 minutes long and has 120 marks. It is worth 25% of the final A-level. The paper is structured as shown in the table below.

Section	Requirements	Marks
A: Religion and ethics	One question from a choice of two; part (a) is AO1 and part (b) is AO2	30 + 30
B: Philosophy of religion	One question from a choice of two; part (a) is AO1 and part (b) is AO2	30 + 30

Year 2

In Year 2 you sit three papers — if you have studied Christianity in Year 1 you can choose between the New Testament paper (Paper 6) and the study of Christianity (Paper 3A). If you studied a different religion, you study Papers 3, 4 and 5.

→ Paper 3 — A study of religion, choosing the same option (religion) as in Year 1.

→ Paper 4 — Religion and ethics

→ Paper 5 — Philosophy of religion

→ Paper 6 — Textual studies (New Testament)

All papers are structured in the same way, as shown in the table below. They are each 1 hour 30 minutes long and have 90 marks. They are worth 20% of the final A-level.

Section	Requirements	Marks
A	One question from a choice of two unified essays	30
B	Two questions from a choice of four unified essays	60

Points to note

→ In Year 1, for Paper 1 you need to spend just over 15 minutes on each essay and for Paper 2 you need to spend about 25 minutes on each essay. In Year 2, you should spend 30 minutes on each essay.

→ It is important to work hard in Year 1 so that you can put that material to one side — and also so that you do not have to answer questions in that style if you have to do a re-sit.

→ Key phrases from the WJEC levels of response descriptors for the top grades include:

  ● Extensive and relevant

  ● Insightful

  ● Confident

  ● Thorough

  ● Perceptive

CCEA

The CCEA exams are offered by the Northern Ireland examination board for students taking exams in Northern Ireland. The key skills of AO1 and AO2 are the same as for the other boards, although they are phrased differently and the exam assessment looks slightly different. Here we summarise how the assessment works if you do the AS and A-level in Years 1 and 2 of your course.

Year 1

In Year 1 you sit two papers from a wide choice of options. Each paper is 1 hour and 20 minutes long and is worth 20% of the final A-level. The papers must be chosen from different sections. The options are:

→ **Section 1: Textual studies**
- AS Paper 1: An introduction to the Gospel of Luke
- AS Paper 2: An introduction to the Acts of the Apostles
- AS Paper 3: An introduction to themes in the Old Testament

→ **Section 2: Systematic study of one religion**
- AS Paper 4: The origins and development of the Early Christian Church to AD 325
- AS Paper 5: The Celtic Church in Ireland in the fifth, sixth and seventh centuries
- AS Paper 6: An introduction to Islam

→ **Section 3: Religion and ethics**
- AS Paper 7: Foundations of ethics with special reference to issues in medical ethics

→ **Section 4: Philosophy of religion**
- AS Paper 8: An introduction to the philosophy of religion

In each exam, one essay is selected from a choice of two in each of the paper's sections A and B. Each essay is split into AO1 and AO2 parts.

Year 2

In Year 2 you sit two papers from a similar choice as in Year 1. Each paper is 2 hours long and is worth 30% of the final A-level. The papers must be chosen from different sections. The options are:

→ **Section 1: Textual studies**
- A2 Paper 1: Themes in the synoptic gospels
- A2 Paper 2: Themes in the selected Letters of St Paul
- A2 Paper 3: Themes in the Old Testament

→ **Section 2: Systematic study of one religion**
- A2 Paper 4: Themes in the early Church and the Church today
- A2 Paper 5: Themes in the Celtic Church, reformation and post-reformation Church
- A2 Paper 6: Islam in a contemporary context

→ **Section 3: Religion and ethics**
- A2 Paper 7: Global ethics

→ **Section 4: Philosophy of religion**
- A2 Paper 8: Themes in the philosophy of religion

In each exam, two essays are chosen from Section A and there is a compulsory question in Section B which tests synoptic links to your other papers. Each essay is split into AO1 and AO2 parts (20 + 30 marks) and should take about 15 minutes for the AO1 part and 25 minutes for the AO2 part.

Points to note

→ It is important in the CCEA A-levels to plan carefully to ensure that you do not run out of time.

→ The BUG technique (see p. 32) will help you to remain focused on the question throughout.

→ Try to avoid the need to do resits by working carefully in Year 1.

→ Key phrases from the CCEA levels of response descriptors for the top grades include:

- Comprehensive understanding
- Sophisticated
- Coherent
- Excellent
- Extensive